Life
in Christ

Also by Jeremy Walker

A Portrait of Paul: Identifying a True Minister of Christ
The Brokenhearted Evangelist
The New Calvinism Considered: A Personal and Pastoral Assessment

Life
in Christ

BECOMING AND BEING
A DISCIPLE OF THE LORD JESUS

Jeremy Walker

REFORMATION HERITAGE BOOKS
Grand Rapids, Michigan

Life in Christ
© 2013 by Jeremy Walker

Reformation Heritage Books
2965 Leonard St. NE
Grand Rapids, MI 49525
616-977-0889 / Fax 616-285-3246
orders@heritagebooks.org
www.heritagebooks.org

Printed in the United States of America
13 14 15 16 17 18/10 9 8 7 6 5 4 3 2 1

ISBN 978-1-60178-274-8 (paperback)
ISBN 978-1-60178-275-5 (epub)

Library of Congress Control Number: 2013952813

For additional Reformed literature, request a free book list from Reformation Heritage Books at the above regular or e-mail address.

CONTENTS

PREFACE

To be a disciple of Jesus Christ is to live in a position of privilege and blessing beyond anything the world might offer. In no part of that life do the children of God ever need to consider themselves apart from the Lord Jesus—nor can they.

My aim in this book is to consider something of the Christian's experience of God's lovingkindness, his sense of God's tender mercies and great goodness, and his relationships with Christ in them and responses to them. Of course it cannot be exhaustive. Who can fully search out unsearchable riches or finally describe an indescribable gift? I hope, though, that it will provide something of a framework for believers, especially those beginning their pilgrimage, enabling them to trace out, understand, enter into, and rejoice over the trajectory of a life in Christ, the ongoing experience of the grace of God toward a sinner.

I hope that this will prove a timely book. Confusion or error with regard to one or a combination of these elements can seriously undermine a Christian's spiritual health, giving him wrong expectations or establishing wrong patterns of conviction and action that ultimately dishonor the God of our salvation, bringing shame on the name of Christ, grieving the Holy Spirit, unsettling and undermining the church, and hamstringing the progress of the gospel.

If we would be healthy, holy, happy saints, then it will do us good to pause and consider the works of God toward us, the blessings bestowed upon us, and our experience of them and responses to them. Salvation is a work in three tenses: we have been saved, we are being saved, and we will be saved. Redemption is a many-sided jewel which delights the soul, not least when it is turned in the light of revelation so that its faces gleam and sparkle before us. The abounding and unending flood of covenant mercies bestowed upon the people of God calls for our close attention, our delighted observation, our earnest praises, and our heartfelt engagement.

It is my sincere prayer that this volume will not only enlighten but also enliven and will both provide believers with scriptural categories by means of which to understand and appreciate their experience, and draw out their hearts toward God in Christ in thankfulness and love for His many mercies toward us.

Chapter 1

LOOKING TO JESUS

*W*e do not begin life as believers in God. No natural heritage or bloodline assures us of a place in the kingdom of God. John tells us that being born of blood, by the will of the flesh, or by the will of man cannot secure our status as children of God (John 1:13). Only by being born of God do we become children of God, and that new birth always manifests itself in receiving the Lord Christ, believing in His name (John 1:12).

That Jeremiah and John the Baptist may have been subject to some degree of saving or sanctifying influence in their mothers' wombs (see Jeremiah 1:5 and Luke 1:41) does not in any way suspend the general principle that "I was brought forth in iniquity, and in sin my mother conceived me" (Ps. 51:5), that my heart and yours are "deceitful above all things, and desperately wicked" (Jer. 17:9), and that "there is none righteous, no, not one" (Rom. 3:10), for "all have sinned and fall short of the glory of God" (Rom. 3:23).

So if we are to have and enjoy life in Christ—not just to understand it in measure but actually to possess it ourselves—we must begin here: "Most assuredly, I say to you, unless one is born again, he cannot see the kingdom of God.... 'You must be born again'" (John 3:3, 7). This is the language of indispensable necessity. No one enters the kingdom without being born from above, without being subject to the enlightening and regenerating influences of the Holy Spirit.

But what is our experience of those influences? What does it feel and look like, and how does it work to be born again?

When the gospel is proclaimed, the commands issued and the invitations given are to believe on the Lord Jesus and to repent of our sins. The Lord Jesus and His disciple John have already made this connection for us. When our Lord says to Nicodemus, and by extension to every one of us, "You must be born again," He is not issuing a command but rather communicating a fact. Being born again is an experience we undergo, not one we initiate or manage. However, our Lord goes on to explain to Nicodemus that "as Moses lifted up the serpent in the wilderness, even so must the Son of Man be lifted up, that whoever believes in Him should not perish but have eternal life" (John 3:14–15). He makes the connections again when He speaks to the crowds in Capernaum, explaining that He is the bread of God from heaven: "All that the Father gives Me will come to Me, and the one who comes to Me I will by no means cast out. For I have come down from heaven, not to do My own will, but the will of Him who sent Me. This is the will of the Father who sent Me, that of all He has given Me I should lose nothing, but should raise it up at the last day" (John 6:37–40). When John writes his gospel, he records the signs Jesus of Nazareth accomplished in order "that you may believe that Jesus is the Christ, the Son of God, and that believing you may have life in His name" (John 20:30–31).

On the day of Pentecost, when Peter proclaimed that God had made this Jesus, whom the people of Jerusalem had crucified, both Lord and Christ, they were cut to the heart and cried out, "Men and brethren, what shall we do?" Peter urged them, "Repent, and let every one of you be baptized in the name of Jesus Christ for the remission of sins; and you shall receive the gift of the Holy Spirit" (Acts 2:36–38). To Cornelius and his household, Peter testifies that to Jesus "all the prophets witness that, through His name, whoever believes in Him will receive remission of sins" (Acts 10:43).

When Paul is preaching at Pisidian Antioch, he declares Jesus as the Christ and then issues an invitation and a warning:

> Therefore let it be known to you, brethren, that through
> this Man is preached to you the forgiveness of sins; and

by Him everyone who believes is justified from all things from which you could not be justified by the law of Moses. Beware therefore, lest what has been spoken in the prophets come upon you:

> *'Behold, you despisers,*
> *Marvel and perish!*
> *For I work a work in your days,*
> *A work which you will by no means believe,*
> *Though one were to declare it to you.'* (Acts 13:38–41)

[handwritten margin note: Apart from regeneration, there is no belief]

When the Gentiles of the city hear this news, "as many as had been appointed to eternal life believed" (Acts 13:48). When Paul is in Athens, he makes the same God known and then makes plain that "these times of ignorance God overlooked, but now commands all men everywhere to repent, because He has appointed a day on which He will judge the world in righteousness by the Man whom He has ordained" (Acts 17:30–31). This he summarizes as declaring "first to those in Damascus and in Jerusalem, and throughout all the region of Judea, and then to the Gentiles, that they should repent, turn to God, and do works befitting repentance" (Acts 26:20).

When the same apostle is explaining the saving effects of and response to the gospel, he says in Romans 10:9–15:

> that if you confess with your mouth the Lord Jesus and believe in your heart that God has raised Him from the dead, you will be saved. For with the heart one believes unto righteousness, and with the mouth confession is made unto salvation. For the Scripture says, "Whoever believes on Him will not be put to shame." For there is no distinction between Jew and Greek, for the same Lord over all is rich to all who call upon Him. For "whoever calls on the name of the LORD shall be saved."
>
> How then shall they call on Him in whom they have not believed? And how shall they believe in Him of whom they have not heard? And how shall they hear without a preacher? And how shall they preach unless they are sent?

I hope you can see and trace the connections. We must be born of God if we are to enter the kingdom: it is an indispensable necessity. But this new birth always results in faith and repentance, and we are never directly commanded to be born again (for that belongs to God) but rather urged by messengers of the gospel of peace to repent of our sins and to turn to God and His Christ in faith, and so obtain everlasting life. That is our experience of this change of heart. The question with us must not first be, "Am I elect?" or "Will I be born again?" but, as we hear the commands and invitations of the gospel, "Am I repenting of my sins and believing in God's Son, Jesus the Christ?" for this is our known and felt experience of salvation.

In that regard, it is no accident that two of the scriptures that the apostle Paul quotes in Romans 10 are drawn from the prophet Isaiah, for Isaiah is a thoroughly and plainly evangelical prophet, a man compelled by God's glory and his own experience of grace to go as a messenger of grace to others. Through him, the Lord is pleased to issue gracious commands and comforts to all who seek peace with Him.

So it is that in Isaiah 45 the Lord God is front and center, revealed as the only living and true God, as the creator and sustainer of all, as the sovereign Lord of heaven and earth, and as the Savior of sinners like us. He is unique. He stands alone, above all idols, He alone being able to deliver:

> They shall be ashamed
> And also disgraced, all of them;
> They shall go in confusion together,
> Who are makers of idols.
> But Israel shall be saved by the LORD
> With an everlasting salvation;
> You shall not be ashamed or disgraced
> Forever and ever. (Isa. 45:16–17)

There is no one like God, none to whom we owe our existence, and none to whom we can look for a blessing. In verse 18

God again speaks as the creator of all things, declaring His utter exclusivity as God and His merciful righteousness:

> *"I am the LORD, and there is no other.*
> *I have not spoken in secret,*
> *In a dark place of the earth;*
> *I did not say to the seed of Jacob,*
> *'Seek Me in vain';*
> *I, the LORD, speak righteousness,*
> *I declare things that are right."* (Isa. 45:18–19)

In verse 21, His exclusivity as Savior now comes to the fore: He says, "There is no other God besides Me, a just God and a Savior; there is none besides Me" (Isa. 45:21). If we know our Bibles, immediately we must hear the voice of God the Son speaking here. Joseph A. Alexander suggests that it is natural for today's readers, who are privileged to know clearly that it is only through the Son that the Father saves, to suppose that it is the pre-incarnate Christ who is speaking here—although it need not have been presumed by the ancient reader.[1] This is the eternal Word by whom the heavens were made, "and all the host of them by the breath of His mouth" (Ps. 33:6). "All things were made through Him, and without Him nothing was made that was made. In Him was life, and the life was the light of men" (John 1:3–4). This is the one who "in the beginning laid the foundation of the earth, and the heavens are the work of [His] hands" (Heb. 1:10). Isaiah saw the glory of Christ and spoke of Him (John 12:41)—that One in whom the Godhead is preeminently made known for salvation.

And it is this One who speaks in rich language, calling to people with words that ring out and echo down through countless gospel sermons through the Scriptures and in history since: "Look to Me, and be saved, all you ends of the earth! For I am God, and there is no other" (Isa. 45:22). Taking this as a prototypical declaration to sinners of God's gospel goodness, let us consider this as Christ's inviting call to believe upon Him and so enter His kingdom and

---

1. Joseph A. Alexander, *Isaiah* (Grand Rapids: Kregel, 1992), 2:188.

the experience of every child of God, to some degree, in hearing and responding to such gracious entreaties.

The Gracious Command and Invitation

First, Christ gives a command: "Look." We have identified this as an inviting call and a gracious entreaty, but we should not overlook the urgency of this word, which comes to us with the force of a divine commandment. There is a wonderful simplicity in this word, and yet it is definite and pointed. The gospel demands engagement. It leaves no neutrals behind. When Paul writes to the Thessalonian Christians about their experience of persecution, he describes their ferocious opponents as those who "do not obey the gospel of our Lord Jesus Christ" (2 Thess. 1:8). In similar fashion, the apostle John records the commandment of God the Father: "that we should believe on the name of His Son Jesus Christ and love one another, as He gave us commandment" (1 John 3:23).

Do not mistake this: the gospel always carries with it the beauty of an invitation and the weight of a command. When someone hears such words, he either receives or rejects the invitation; he obeys or disobeys the command. Such exhortations and encouragements never leave us in no-man's-land but either draw us to the side of Christ or disclose our distance from or antipathy to Him.

When an awakened sinner hears such words as these, under the influence of the Spirit he feels at least something of their majesty, their compelling force, and their divine authority and understands something of their consuming demand. For what is commanded here is a distinctive way of looking. Here the living Lord requires us to look *from* something *to* something else. It is a cry to detach our thoughts, concerns, hopes, and desires from whatever distractions and deviations they have been running after and turn our full attention to some other thing. Whatever we might have been pursuing, we are to leave it and pursue something else entirely. The fact that this is a command demonstrates that it is not something to be trifled with. The nature of the demand shows that it calls for a wholehearted seeking after something, turning our whole attention from all other things into a particular channel.

This is not a command that depends upon our physical capacities, as if the farsighted or nearsighted, or even the altogether blind, are somehow disbarred. Indeed, it is notable in Mark's gospel, for example, that blind Bartimaeus sees far more clearly and looks far more intently than multitudes with 20/20 vision. He will not stop shouting until he has gained the attention of Jesus of Nazareth: "Son of David, have mercy on me!" (Mark 10:46–52).

This commands the looking that saves—a willing for, wishing for, desiring after, trusting in, taking hold of, hanging on to, and hoping in Jesus Christ, the Son of God, the Savior of sinners. This is language that would have chimed with Simeon, that "just and devout" man who was "waiting for the Consolation of Israel." He was waiting to see the Lord's Christ. He had given this his full attention, and when he saw the infant Christ he declared that now he had set eyes upon that for which he had long been looking:

> *For my eyes have seen Your salvation*
> *Which You have prepared before the face of all peoples,*
> *A light to bring revelation to the Gentiles,*
> *And the glory of Your people Israel.* (Luke 2:25–32)

When ancient Anna arrived, "in that instant she gave thanks to the Lord, and spoke of Him to all those who *looked for* redemption in Jerusalem" (Luke 2:38, emphasis added). These faithful people did not hang around in the vague hope of seeing something. They saw that for which—that One for whom—they had long been looking and waiting: the Lord's Christ. They were obeying this command.

How sweet and simple this is, but how much it humbles us, bringing down all our high ideas of self, pointing us away from ourselves and our own notions of capacity and worthiness. So often this leaves us like Naaman, told by Elisha's servant to go and wash seven times in the Jordan in order to be restored from his leprosy and made clean.

But Naaman became furious, and went away and said, "Indeed, I said to myself, 'He will surely come out to me, and stand and call on the name of the LORD his God, and wave his hand over the place, and heal the leprosy.' Are not the Abanah and the Pharpar, the rivers of Damascus, better than all the waters of Israel? Could I not wash in them and be clean?" So he turned and went away in a rage. (2 Kings 5:11–12)

Naaman had big ideas of his own importance and firm notions of the worthiness of his own resources. He needed to be humbled by those faithful servants of his who asked if—given that he would have done something great, if required, in order to be healed—he would not now do this simple thing: "Wash, and be clean" (2 Kings 5:13).

In similar fashion, such a command as this turns us out and away from ourselves and from our own notions of helping ourselves and sends us to another. It is a call to faith, and saving faith, in its essence, sends us out of and away from ourselves. But it would be a counsel of despair if the Lord did not also identify an object for our looking: "Look to Me."

Faith does not operate in a vacuum. Faith always has an object, and the Lord does not leave us wondering where or to whom we must look in matters of such importance. To do so would leave us as lost, bewildered, and confused as ever we were. Christ says, "Look to Me—turn from all else and all others beside, and, in this matter of your salvation, look always and only to Me."

Do not look to any other creature, to men or to angels, as if there were merit enough in any or all of them to move you one inch closer to God. Do not look to idols, to the vain imaginations of human fantasy or the pointless creations of human ingenuity, so often proposed and received as things worthy of trust. Do not look to your own works; do not look to your own tears and repenting; do not look to your own heart and emotions; do not look to your graces and gifts in their exercise and operation. Do not look to your religious rites, ceremonies, and observances. Do not look to your

mysticism

would-be holy feasts and festivals. Do not look to your own righteousness, your own efforts, to make you acceptable with the Holy One of Israel, for that will not qualify you. Indeed, in one sense sin is the only qualification we need, and it is one which we have in a horrible abundance.

The command comes to us as sinners and tells us to turn away from all these things and look to the Christ of God; the Son of God; the Lamb of God who takes away the sin of the world; the one Mediator between God and men, the man Christ Jesus; the only Savior of sinners; the sole Redeemer of the lost.

We look to Him at Calvary. There hangs the suffering, bleeding, dying Lamb. Look to Him, with the crown of thorns piercing His noble brow. Look to Him, with the blood pouring from His hands and feet, cruelly pierced with Roman nails. Look to Him as the gore drips from His wounded flesh, torn from His back by a vicious scourge. Look to Him as He bows His head in agony under the weight of His holy Father's just anger against sin. Look to Him as He cries out from the midst of an impenetrable darkness, "My God, My God, why have you forsaken Me?" Look to Him as He shouts with a loud voice, "It is finished!" Look to Him as He yields up His Spirit.

This is the cry to which faith wholeheartedly responds, and to which faith, so looking, is able to say:

> *See there the meek, expiring Lamb!*
> *'Tis finished! He expires for me.*[2]

The great theologian John Owen makes this point in a rich passage on the nature of faith, relentlessly seeking to communicate the nature of this forceful invitation and the right response to it.[3] He says, first, that the faith by which a sinner is justified is most frequently expressed in the New Testament as *receiving*. It is, says

---

2. Charles Wesley, "'Tis Finished! The Messiah Dies."
3. What follows is essentially a recasting of *The Doctrine of Justification by Faith*, by John Owen, in *The Works of John Owen* (Edinburgh: Banner of Truth, 1965), 5:291–94.

Owen, Christ Himself that we receive: "But as many as received Him, to them He gave the right to become children of God, to those who believe in His name" (John 1:12). Unbelief is, therefore, not receiving Christ (John 1:11; 3:11; 12:48; 14:17). Faith receives Christ as the One who is made by God to be "THE LORD OUR RIGHTEOUSNESS" (Jer. 23:6; 33:16). In looking to and receiving Christ for salvation, neither grace nor duty cooperates with faith; only faith so grasps the Lord Jesus, and nothing else is involved. In addition, this receiving Christ as our saving righteousness utterly excludes any other righteousness but His from our justification; we are "justified by faith." Faith alone receives Christ, and Christ, as received by faith, is the cause and basis of our justification. It is only in this way that we become the sons of God. So we receive the reconciliation made by the blood of Christ (Rom. 5:11), whom God set forth as a propitiation by His blood, through faith (Rom. 3:25). In receiving this reconciling atonement, the believing and repenting sinner thoroughly and willingly approves of and assents to Christ's bloody death as the only way of salvation and appropriates that sacrifice to himself. In doing so, we receive the forgiveness of sins: "that they may receive forgiveness of sins and an inheritance among those who are sanctified by faith in Me" (Acts 26:18). In receiving Christ we receive the atonement, and in the atonement we receive the forgiveness of sins.

Even the "abundance of grace" and "the gift of righteousness" (Rom. 5:17) (righteousness considered as the efficient and material cause of our justification) are received in this way. Faith, operating like this, receives everything that lies behind and gives rise to God's declaration that we are righteous in His sight.

Having emphasized that faith involves receiving the merits of another and in itself merits nothing, Owen then explores other language, turning to Isaiah 45:22 to explain that faith is also expressed by *looking*: "Look to Me, and be saved" (he also points to Isaiah 17:7; Zechariah 12:10; and Psalm 123:2). We see the nature of this looking, according to Owen, in John 3: "And as Moses lifted up the serpent in the wilderness, even so must the Son of Man be

[handwritten margin notes: Faith – receiving / coming / fleeing]

lifted up, that whoever believes in Him should not perish but have eternal life" (vv. 14–15). These verses refer to Christ being lifted up to die on the cross (John 8:28; 12:32). The fiery creatures and the death that followed their attack are clearly, for Owen, representative of the guilt of sin and the lawful punishment that follows (1 Cor. 10:11). He explores the parallels: when someone was bitten *[margin: Moses]* and sought any remedies apart from the one that God had provided, he perished. Only those who looked to the bronze serpent *[margin: serpent]* that was lifted up were healed and lived. This was what God had ordained, the one appointed way in which those people could be healed. And here we have pictured the pardon of sin and the grant of everlasting life. *[margin: shadow / Christ / Calvary]*

In this way of looking we have portrayed the nature of faith, as our Savior makes clear: "Even so must the Son of Man be lifted up, that whoever believes in Him"—that is, whoever looks to Him in the same way that the Israelites in the wilderness looked to the bronze serpent—"should not perish but have eternal life" (John 3:14–15).

So faith, justification, and salvation are made clear to us through this scriptural, historical illustration. If the faith that justifies, in principle and practice, involves the lost and guilty sinner looking to Christ alone for everything he needs by way of help—for deliverance, righteousness, and life—then it is clear that nothing else is involved in our being justified. And this is just what happens when a sinner is converted: faith is the act of the soul by which those who are hopeless, helpless, and lost in themselves expectantly and believingly seek after all the help and relief they need in Christ alone.

By now, of course, Owen is hitting his stride, and so he begins to explore this grace of faith, turning it this way and that, letting the light reflect off it as it is described in the Scriptures. So we find that it is often called a *coming to Christ*: "Come to Me, all you who labor and are heavy laden, and I will give you rest" (Matt. 11:28; cf. John 6:35, 37, 45, 65; 7:37). To come to Christ for life and salvation is to believe on Him with an eye to the justification of life (no other grace or duty, but faith only, is coming to Christ like this, and therefore everything but faith is excluded from this matter of justification). Ask someone who has been convinced of sin and weary of its burden, who has determined to flee from the wrath to come and has heard the voice of Christ in the gospel inviting him to come unto Him for help and relief. That person, by the Spirit's illumination, will tell you that coming to Christ in this way involves going out of and turning away from yourself, completely renouncing all your own duties and righteousness, and applying yourself with all your trust and confidence to Christ alone, resorting only to His righteousness to be pardoned for sin, accepted with God, and granted a right to the heavenly inheritance.

Faith is sometimes expressed in the language of *fleeing* for refuge: Christians "have fled for refuge to lay hold of the hope set before us" (Heb. 6:18; cf. Prov. 18:10). Faith might be defined, then, as the flight of the soul to Christ to be delivered from sin and misery. Again, this assumes that someone is already convinced of his lost condition, and, if nothing changes, there is only damnation to come. Such a person is convinced that he cannot deliver himself from this doom and must look elsewhere for deliverance. He therefore considers Christ as set before him and offered to him in the promise of the gospel. Persuaded that this is the only holy and safe way—a way characterized by divine excellence in every part—to be delivered from death and find acceptance with God, the sinner flees immediately and sincerely to Christ for refuge in order not to perish in his present condition. He trusts in God's provision entirely and alone.

Elsewhere in the Old Testament we find faith expressed in terms of *leaning on God* (Mic. 3:11) or *Christ* (Song 8:5); *rolling* or *casting ourselves and our burden on the Lord* (Pss. 22:8; 37:5); *resting on* or *in God* (2 Chron. 14:11; Ps. 37:7); *clinging, holding fast to,* or *continuing with the Lord* (Deut. 4:4; Acts 11:23); or, in countless places, *trusting, hoping,* and *waiting.*[4]

---

4. The eighteenth-century Dutch Further Reformation divine Alexander

faith

Here, then, is a rich biblical vocabulary of turning away from ourselves in dependence on another: receiving, looking, coming, fleeing, leaning, rolling, or casting ourselves and our burden on another, resting, cleaving or clinging, trusting, hoping, and waiting. And so, concludes Owen,

> It may be observed, that those who acted in faith as it is thus expressed, do everywhere declare themselves to be lost, hopeless, helpless, desolate, poor, orphans; whereon they place all their hope and expectation on God alone.
>
> All that I would infer from these things is, that the faith whereby we believe unto the justification of life, or which is required of us in a way of duty that we may be justified, is such an act of the whole soul whereby convinced sinners do wholly go out of themselves to rest upon God in Christ for mercy, pardon, life, righteousness, and salvation, with an acquiescence of heart therein; which is the whole of the truth pleaded for.[5]

This, then, is what we are commanded to do when the Lord calls to us, "Look!" Despairing of ourselves, we look to Christ alone in dependent faith and developing adoration as He suffered and died in the place of sinners, and in doing so we are saved.

The Glorious Purpose and Promise — *To be saved!*

This is the glorious purpose intended and a glorious promise held out. Why are we directed so to look to Jesus Christ? To what end are we so commanded? It is in order that we might be saved. "Look to Me," says the Lord of glory, "and you will be saved."

Note the certainty. Only look, only rest in Christ, turning to Him with faith, and you will be saved. Do you doubt that it will be so? "Look to Me and be saved...for I am God and there is no

① certain ② immediate ③ complete

Comrie devoted an entire book, *The ABC of Faith* (Grand Rapids: Netherlands Reformed Book and Publishing, 2011), to expounding twenty-eight synonyms that Scripture uses for faith's coming to Christ.

5. Owen, *Justification by Faith*, 5:294.

other." This is not only a declaration of the Redeemer's inherent ability to be true to His word but also a statement of His divine obligation to act upon His promise. Think of it: if the Lord turns away the penitent, trusting sinner, He undoes Himself! He ceases to be the God of mercy and truth. He will not deny the one who comes to Him; the repenting, returning, believing sinner will by no means be cast out (John 6:37).

Note also the immediacy. It almost takes less time to do than to say it! The effect is instant. It may be that for a long time, a sinner has wrestled with his felt unworthiness to come to Christ. It may be that he has long doubted whether Christ is willing to save him. But he has been irresistibly drawn and effectually called, and so he comes, and he looks, and in that moment he is saved. What a marvel of grace this is, that we might be sitting one moment a wretched, lost man or woman, dead in trespasses and sins, altogether filthy. But the Spirit has been at work in us, and our eyes are now open to behold the glory of God shining in the face of Jesus Christ, and in that moment of true seeing we are truly saved. From out of the dominion of darkness we are carried, translated in that moment into the kingdom of the Son of God's love. That is the moment in which we experience salvation, however clearly we are able to discern it and whether our sense of it is more like that of a tipping point in the entrance of light (like Lydia, for example) or more like the flashing of lightning (like the Philippian jailer, perhaps).

And consider, too, the fullness of it, the completeness of it. This is no halfway house. There is no probationary period. If we have looked, we are saved, and our lives are hidden with Christ in God. You cannot be a little bit saved. This is salvation complete in degree and extent. I am not suggesting that you cannot enjoy a fuller experience of what it means to be saved, but I am adamant that you cannot be more saved than you are in the moment at which you look to Jesus, and you cannot become saved and then cease to be saved. Remember Isaiah 45:17—when God saves, He saves with an everlasting salvation, in which there is not and never can be the least degree of shame or disgrace.

Again, this is the decree of the sovereign, saving God: "Who has declared this from ancient time? Who has told it from that time? Have not I, the LORD?" (Isa. 45:21). One moment, the sinner was teetering on the brink of an eternity in hell, the next he is snatched by grace to a life of joy unspeakable and full of glory, thankful praise, and mercies temporal and eternal that all the tribulations in this fallen and hostile world cannot sweep away, to a taste of glory here and an eternal heaven with God hereafter.

There is no other salvation, certainly no better, for there is no other God. All sinners, if they are to be saved, must be saved by this God in this way. The richest people in the world and the poorest beggars on the street must all alike be saved by turning from their sins to trust in this Jesus. The most brilliant philosophers and scholars and the slowest learners are leveled here. The greatest wits and artists and the untaught child who cannot read or write a word come in the same rank. The most respectable and outwardly upright pillars of society and the lowest, vilest, most degraded outcasts must all be saved by looking to Jesus to save them from their sins.

Truly these things crush all high thoughts of self:

> Perish each thought of human pride,
> Let God alone be magnified.[6]

If you will not look to Christ, then you cannot be saved. If you have not looked to Christ, then you are not saved. But if you will look to Christ, you must be saved. If you have looked to Christ, you are saved.

But there is something else worth seeing here, for there are many who doubt this offer. Some torture themselves with fears that perhaps, after all, they were not included in this grand invitation or encompassed by this gracious command. It is one of those declarations that is almost beyond belief, and yet there is a richness here that we have not yet touched upon.

It lies in the promise extended to "all you ends of the earth" (Isa. 45:22). At this point, many of the Jews of Isaiah's day—those who

---

6. Philip Doddridge, "God of Salvation, We Adore."

drew near to God with their mouths but not their hearts—would have been dumbfounded and offended: "Surely we shall be saved, but not any Gentile scum!" In Christ's day, the Pharisees would, perhaps, have had all but themselves consigned to hell. Even after Christ's death and resurrection and that Great Commission, which sent the disciples to make disciples of all the nations, we find Peter balking at the breadth of the invitation. Are we any less prone than Peter to err in this regard?

Do we sometimes say these words, or words like them, and mean, "Look to Christ and be saved…all you pleasant people, all you people of a certain educational or social standard, all you people who look like you might fit neatly into our congregation, all you people of a certain race or color, all you people of a certain background, all you people of a certain status and standing, all you people of a certain appearance, all you people who have attained a certain level of respectability"?

If we say it, suggest it, or hint it, we are blasphemously misquoting the God of salvation, who says, "Look to Me and be saved, *all you ends of the earth.*" God has no qualms in issuing this invitation. There is a geographical and spiritual universalism here that excludes none: "Go into all the world and preach the gospel to every creature." Christ has purchased a people for Himself, paying for them with His own precious blood, but they are now scattered through every culture and society and throughout all their parts and levels. The church and her ministers—"those who preach the gospel of peace, who bring glad tidings of good things" (Rom. 10:9–15)—are sent to

> *Publish abroad*
> *Again and again*
> *The Son's glorious merit,*
> *The Father's free grace,*
> *The gift of the Spirit,*
> *To Adam's lost race.*[7]

---

7. Joseph Hart, "Give Glory to God, Ye Children of Men."

The church is to believe this promise, both for ourselves—we are to trust Him exclusively—and for others—we are to offer Him universally. We are to put no human limitation on divine redemption. Christ makes no exceptions: He says to any sinner, man or woman, boy or girl, "Look to Me and be saved." We are not to refuse Christ because of our sin when Christ has not refused us on account of it. It is sinners whom Christ has come to save.

It may be that you do not yet have life in Christ. It may be you have tried a thousand different ways to obtain peace with God. You might have a mind full of the foulness of your soul, the lightness of your sense of sin, the horrors that you have spoken, thought, or done, but Christ does not hold you at arm's length. He Himself bids you come. He Himself offers you everlasting salvation, saying, "Look to Me and be saved." All who have looked to Christ have been and are being saved and have never been shamed or disappointed. If we say we cannot look, we must cry to the God who gives grace to the humble, who grants grace for looking. We are to look—and leave the saving to a sovereign and merciful God.

And if we have looked, then we live. This is our passage from death to life, from darkness to light, when we believe on the Son of God. This is our first breath of new life. This is the proof that God is at work in our hearts, when, with newly opened eyes, we gaze with repenting faith upon the Son of God in all His saving glory, and—believing—enter into the family of God. This is life in Christ.

Trust God exclusively;
Offer Him universally.

For Further Reflection

1. Have you now or in the past assumed that being born into a family with Christian parents, being baptized or sprinkled or christened, or having always attended a church where the gospel is proclaimed automatically makes you a Christian? Why is this a dangerous and even deadly assumption?

2. Describe, using biblical language, what is necessary for a sinner to enter God's kingdom. What is a Christian's experience of this? What does someone do when this happens to him or her?

3. Have you reckoned with the fact that God's gospel is both invitation and command? What does this mean for you and others?

4. What or who is the object of saving faith? What else are we tempted to look to? What, specifically, have you been or are you tempted to look to?

5. Briefly describe faith—the "looking" of Isaiah 45:22—by some of its parallel biblical expressions. Which of these do you find sweetest, most helpful, most comforting?

6. The salvation that God promises is certain, immediate, and complete. What effect should that have on you if you want to be or are a Christian?

7. Does the broadness and freeness of God's offer of salvation unsettle you or trouble you in any way? Why might that be? Should it be so?

8. What advice would you give to someone who wanted to be converted and become a Christian?

Chapter 2

UNITED TO CHRIST

*W*hen the Puritan John Flavel wrote about keeping our hearts, he began in this typically vigorous and direct way:

The greatest difficulty in conversion is to win the heart to God, and the greatest difficulty after conversion is to keep the heart with God.... "Keep your heart with all diligence." ...Lavater[1] suggests that the word is taken from a besieged garrison, surrounded by many enemies without and in danger of being betrayed by treacherous citizens within. Given this danger the soldiers are commanded to watch, upon pain of death. And while the expression ["keep your heart"] seems to make this our responsibility, yet it does not imply a sufficiency or ability in us to do it. We are as able to stop the sun in its course, or to make the rivers run backward, as by our own skill and power to rule and order our hearts. We may as well be our own *saviours*, as our own *keepers*. And yet Solomon speaks accurately enough when he says, "keep your heart," because the duty is ours although the power is God's. A natural man has no power; a gracious man has some, though not enough; and whatever power he has depends on the invigorating and assisting strength of Christ. Grace within us is indebted to grace without us: "Without me you can do nothing (John 15:5)."[2]

---

1. Ludwig Lavater (1527–1586) was a Swiss Reformed theologian related by marriage to and associated with Heinrich Bullinger.

2. John Flavel, *A Saint Indeed*, in *The Works of John Flavel* (Edinburgh: Banner of Truth, 1968), 5:423–24. I have updated the language and grammar.

The saved sinner is a person under assault. People often mistakenly assume that conversion means an end to spiritual battles. Although God in His mercy often grants the new believer a period of respite from strife and abounding joy, there is a real sense in which conversion is not so much the end of our battles as their beginning.

In writing to the church at Corinth, Paul was addressing an assaulted congregation, under attack from the world, the flesh, and the devil. At this church false teachers have not so much crept in as strutted and been welcomed in, and one of Paul's aims in writing his second letter to the Corinthians is to show them their folly and establish them in some of those fundamental realities under threat from false instruction and flawed assumption.

In 2 Corinthians 5, Paul deals with the need for all believers to live in a manner well pleasing to God, assured of the resurrection to come, and then he turns his guns against the false teachers "who boast in appearance and not in heart" (v. 12). The apostle is not so much concerned to vindicate himself as the gospel he preaches, and he does this by setting forth positive truths and their consequences.

One of his primary thrusts in the latter part of the chapter is the consequences of a Christian's identification with Christ in His death and resurrection:

> For the love of Christ compels us, because we judge thus: that if One died for all, then all died; and He died for all, that those who live should live no longer for themselves, but for Him who died for them and rose again. (2 Cor. 5:14–15)

There are consequences that flow from such accurate judgment:

> Therefore, from now on, we regard no one according to the flesh. Even though we have known Christ according to the flesh, yet now we know Him thus no longer. Therefore, if anyone is in Christ, he is a new creation; old things have passed away; behold, all things have become new. (2 Cor. 5:16–17)

He makes the point with equal clarity in other places. For example, in Romans 6 he asks, "What shall we say then?" to the suggestion that we can go on living as we once did, or perhaps even should continue to live, in order that God's grace may be exalted. "Shall we continue in sin that grace may abound?" His answer is unequivocal, grounded in the realities of our identification with Christ in His death and resurrection:

> Certainly not! How shall we who died to sin live any longer in it? Or do you not know that as many of us as were baptized into Christ Jesus were baptized into His death?...
>
> Now if we died with Christ, we believe that we shall also live with Him, knowing that Christ, having been raised from the dead, dies no more. Death no longer has dominion over Him. For the death that He died, He died to sin once for all; but the life that He lives, He lives to God. Likewise you also, reckon yourselves to be dead indeed to sin, but alive to God in Christ Jesus our Lord.
>
> Therefore do not let sin reign in your mortal body, that you should obey it in its lusts. And do not present your members as instruments of unrighteousness to sin, but present yourselves to God as being alive from the dead, and your members as instruments of righteousness to God. For sin shall not have dominion over you, for you are not under law but under grace. (Rom. 6:1–3, 8–14)

In Galatians 6 he says, "God forbid that I should boast except in the cross of our Lord Jesus Christ, by whom the world has been crucified to me, and I to the world. For in Christ Jesus neither circumcision nor uncircumcision avails anything, but a new creation" (vv. 14–15). Again, the emphasis is on our identity as those who—being united to Christ—are new creations in Him. We are crucified to the world and the world to us: the cross of the Savior casts its pall in both directions, so that the world loses its sparkle in our eyes, and we have no beauty in the eyes of the world. As such, we no longer live for ourselves, but for Him who died for us and rose again (2 Cor. 5:15). In 2 Corinthians, Paul goes on to point out that he is past judging by external appearances as the false teachers require and do; no one is regarded or assessed according to the flesh, the outer man. Even Christ is no longer thought of as the world (and Paul) once knew Him—lowly, despised, forsaken—but as He is in truth: glorified, exalted, triumphant, reigning, saving with power.

From these truths Paul draws a conclusion, namely, that "if anyone is in Christ, he is a new creation; old things have passed away; behold, all things have become new" (2 Cor. 5:17). Here is the first and greatest part of Flavel's answer to the conundrum of keeping the heart: the duty is ours, though the power is of God. A natural man has no power; a gracious man has some, though not sufficient, and what power he does have depends upon "the exciting and assisting strength of Christ." Grace within us is indebted to grace without us; without Christ you can do nothing.

As one who has looked to Christ and been saved, Paul presses home a Christian's identity in Christ, observing his position and nature and then giving an explanation or exposition of those realities.

The Position Described

"If anyone is in Christ." You will immediately notice the breadth of this statement. It applies to any and all who can legitimately be described as "in Christ." There is no difference or distinction with regard to physical age or spiritual maturity, gender, previous religious affiliation, history of transgression, depth or extent of true religious knowledge, or anything else by which we tend to judge and rank one another. All those who have looked to Christ Jesus and been saved are on the same level with one another. With regard to what follows, all believers—all those "in Christ"—are as one.

This is often a battle for believers; the problem may be not so much that others judge us to be somehow in the second rank as that we are slow to believe what is spoken concerning us. But there are no Christians who need to exclude themselves from this. Sometimes our enemy is confusion: we might have been told that there are some believers who attain to a higher plane of spiritual reality. Perhaps we fight pride, often in the form of a sort of inverted or perverted humility, as if we are somehow the exception to a general rule, the only saint in the history of the world who might not be able to say this of himself. But we must not exclude or isolate ourselves.

There are no exceptions to this Christian rule, and—if we make ourselves that exception or allow ourselves to be excepted— then we might end up deliberately or unintentionally denying our blessings or avoiding our duties. For some immature or confused Christians, a denial of basic spiritual realities can become an excuse not to pursue those standards established for us in the Word of God. "After all," we might ask, "if I am not *this*, how can I be expected to pursue *that*?" So we cut the nerve of godliness and allow ourselves to live at a low ebb because we have told ourselves that we have no basis on which to expect anything different. Equally, we can cut ourselves off from the blessings and privileges to which we are genuinely entitled by our status in Christ Jesus, feeling ourselves unworthy of them (we are) and concluding that we are therefore excluded from them (we are not). Again, the effect is to deaden us, leaving us at a felt distance from God in Christ and despairing of any progress in godliness because of the mistaken assumption that we are somehow not in possession of the relationships or realities upon which that progress is grounded.

However, Paul is speaking here of every true Christian—none, thank God, are exempt! So let us look more carefully at the position of the person that Paul is describing. He is "in Christ." This is just another way of describing a Christian.

There are three possible relationships that a person might sustain to the Lord Christ. First, someone might be *without Christ.* This is our state by nature. It is how we came into this world before we looked to Christ, perhaps before we even knew that there was a Christ to look to. A person might have been born into the greatest nation and richest city, gifted with a high-grade brain and a beautiful face and a naturally attractive body, even into a home with Christian parents, but he is born without Christ. No number of earthly privileges can change that fact. We can be subjects of

1) without Christ - nature   3) in Christ
2) with Christ - glory

monarchs with religious roles and titles, citizens of nations with a grand heritage healthily tinged with Christian morality, and can attend the most orthodox church and hear intelligent and impassioned preaching week by week and still be without Christ. To lack food is terrible; to lack money is distressing; to lack health is miserable; to lack friends is tragic; but to lack Christ is to lack the greatest and most necessary good—it is the most awful situation imaginable. If we had Christ, all else could be borne, but to live and die without Christ makes any number of other blessings little better than dust and ashes in our mouths.

Second, someone might be *with Christ.* If to be without Christ is the height of woe, then to be with Christ is the pinnacle of bliss, for this is the very joy and blessing of glory. To be "present with the Lord" (2 Cor. 5:8) is the heaven of heaven. There is no greater joy, no happier prospect, no sweeter moment than to have the eye actually rest upon the Lord Christ, the glorified Savior of sinners. This is the anticipation of the dying saint, the prospect for the resurrection that makes every other hint of the glory to come shine with golden light. However, if we are to be with Christ when we die or taken to be with Him when He returns, we need to bear in mind that no one will ever be with Christ unless they are first in Christ.

And that is our third category, the one that Paul addresses here: *in Christ.* It is the very opposite of being "in Adam" (Rom. 5:12–21), which we are by nature. It is very different from being "in the world," which we are by sinful inclination. It is not the same as being "in church"—there are many people who imagine that being in a church building from time to time, in regular attendance at church services, or even a member of some church, even one where the truth is preached, will somehow of itself guarantee their salvation. You can be in church and without Christ.

To be "in Christ" is to be savingly united to the Lord Jesus Christ by faith. It is a saving connection to the Lord, God's gracious gift to otherwise hopeless sinners, granted in sovereign mercy. To be in Christ is to know the certainty of being "accepted in the Beloved" (Eph. 1:6), readily received and embraced by the Father on account of the Son in all His perfections. It is to be secure, nourished, and assured of the life which is to come. A Christian is in Christ in the same way that a hand or foot is in the body: God "gave Him to be head over all things to the church, which is His body, the fullness of Him who fills all in all" (Eph. 1:22–23).

This is the sure result of looking to Him and being saved, the certain consequence of entrusting your soul to Him. We get to be in Christ by faith and with love: by faith, when we depend utterly upon Him alone to make us acceptable in the sight of the holy God, and with love when we adore Him above all and any others, as the true joy of our hearts. Where faith is sincere, love will readily follow. We are in Christ in the same way that Noah was in the ark: in a place of safety, peace, and rest, shut in by the very hand of God Himself and made secure against all the terrors of law and judgment. To be "in Christ" is—in the very instant in which that is true—to be the inheritor of all that Jesus accomplished by His atoning death and glorious resurrection. By the time Paul died, he had spent long, faithful, fruitful years "in Christ." When the thief on the cross died, he had spent a few agonizing, helpless hours "in Christ." But neither was more or less in Christ; neither was more or less righteous in God's eyes; neither was more or less beloved of God for Christ's sake. It is being "in Christ" that makes all the difference to any man or woman and paves the way to be with Christ when He returns or takes us home. This is true for anyone who is in Christ, and Paul now goes on to explain something about the nature of such a person.

The Nature Identified

creation, not mere transformation

"If anyone is in Christ," writes the apostle, "he is a new creation." This is the language of a *radical change*. It speaks of something not simply different but genuinely new. It is not enough to speak of a tadpole becoming a frog or a caterpillar becoming a butterfly, for the language of transformation and metamorphosis falls short of the reality. Even the Ethiopian changing the rich color of his skin or the leopard changing his distinctive spots is insufficient. This is not alteration but creation, newness at the deepest level.

It speaks of a *thorough change*. It deals not with appearance but with nature. If the Ethiopian could change his skin color, he would remain an Ethiopian. If the leopard could alter his spots, he would still be a leopard. But the new creation begins at and radiates from the core of a person's being and changes everything he is. It starts with the inner man enthroning Christ in the heart, the seat of the government of our humanity, and begins its course there, creating anew from that point outward, nothing being overlooked or bypassed, all being more or less affected and increasingly renovated over time.

This, then, is a *divinely worked change*, accomplished by nothing less than heavenly power. Mere mortal strength could never begin or sustain such a work—human might and ingenuity can no more create a person anew than it can truly create anything to begin with. And, indeed, there is a sense in which this act of salvation transcends even the act of original creation. In creation, God worked from nothing. In salvation, He worked against sin. In the Scriptures, the heavens are considered to be the work of God's fingers (Ps. 8:3) but the saints are redeemed by the exercise of His strong right hand (Pss. 44:3; 98:1; cf. Deut. 9:29). Even the sinner's very desire to be saved is given by God! "The carnal mind is enmity against God" (Rom. 8:7): it fights and despises God and desires its own will and way. Yet God comes and creates a new heart that turns to Christ; thus, the Lord replaces the carnal mind with a spiritual one, earthly appetites with heavenly ones, a manward attitude with a Godward. He does not work against our will in salvation, but He makes the will fresh, so that it can be said of the one "in Christ" that "he is a new creation"—finding his identity in an uncontaminated work of God.

The union that a saved sinner has by faith with the Lord Christ is a transforming union. Whoever is in Christ is a new creation; these realities belong invariably together. There is a radical, fundamental, thorough, divinely worked act of new creation that occurs in the life of the man or woman who is brought into Christ. Professing Christians who are no different from what they were before an alleged conversion are no true Christians at all. The fundamental change, however slowly its effects may fully penetrate the whole, is real and definite; it is there, and nothing is the same.

This new creation outdoes anything that the world has to offer. Educators, politicians, mystics, medics, moralists, philosophers, spiritualists, scientists—all claim, one way or another, to be able to change things, to improve, to upgrade, to rehabilitate mankind. But only the Holy Spirit can regenerate a person, only in Christ can it truly be said of a person that "he is a new creation." This is not a new angle, not a new brand, not a new approach, not a new policy, not a new system—but a new nature.

It may, though, be worth noting that being "in Christ" and being "a new creation" cannot be separated. Paul does not say that if anyone is a new creation, he therefore has some claim on Christ. Rather, the reality of the new creation hinges on the relationship to Christ. Some might say, "I do not think that I am strong enough to live as a new creation. I am not sure I could fulfill the obligations, live up to the standards, stand up to the opposition, and put to death my sins." But this is to put the cart before the horse. Our concern is first to be "in Christ" by faith—the realities of the new creation depend upon that relationship. No one is able to do these things out of Christ. A person cannot re-create himself. The Spirit gives a new heart which turns to Christ in faith, and—in union with Jesus—the sin-sick sinner can be described as a new creation. But how does this work out? What does it look like in practice?

The Explanation Supplied

Paul does not leave this statement standing beautiful but bald before us. He expounds it for us in terms of a Christian's experience of life in Christ: "Old things have passed away; behold, all things have become new." Although it may not be immediately evident from the English translation, there are two significantly different senses here. Perhaps we could more accurately put it this

way: "The old has gone and is gone for good; the new has come
and keeps on coming."

"The old has gone and is gone for good." We know that the
body does not immediately change—our external features remain
fundamentally the same—but Paul has already pointed out that
we do not judge by such things anyway. No, what has passed away
is the old man. The child of God can say, in effect, "I used to live
for myself, but now I have been crucified to the world and to self.
I have been crucified with Christ, and I no longer live, but Christ
lives in me. The life that I live in the body I live by faith in the Son
of God, who loved me and gave Himself for me" (cf. Gal. 2:20;
6:14). The old treasures no longer sparkle. The old affections, passions, desires, appetites, aims, hopes, and priorities have had the
axe laid to the root. They no longer govern us, and our fundamental allegiance to the things of the world has been severed. As a
Christian, I am no longer under the reign of sin and the dominion
of Satan—I am a new man in Christ Jesus: "God be thanked that
though you were slaves of sin, yet you obeyed from the heart that
form of doctrine to which you were delivered. And having been set
free from sin, you became slaves of righteousness" (Rom. 6:17–18).
I do not mean by this that there are no more battles to fight, but
that we have changed sides.

Have you ever seen this? Have you perhaps witnessed it in
your home, in a church, in the life of a friend? I trust that you can
identify it in yourself. There is that ill-tempered teenage girl who
comes to church because she has to, her hair hanging down over
her face to avoid meeting anyone's eye; her face set in a permanent sulk; her shoulders hunched against contact with people; her
clothes, make-up, and jewelry all sending the message, "I do what
I want when I choose." Then one day she is sitting under the gospel with a clear eye—perhaps even a visible pair of eyes—with her
shoulders back, her face open, her body relaxed, her mouth smiling, engaging with the truth.

There is that vicious lad, hanging out on the street corners,
picking up an increasingly troubling criminal record, running with

a pack of others as seemingly feral as himself, set against his distant family, dismissed as worthless by his teachers, in continual conflict with all authority, a true dead-ender if ever there were one. He is found walking away from the life of godlessness, the criminal record has come to an abrupt halt, the attitude to authority has shifted, he begins to pay attention to what is spoken and taught, and now his parents are more confused by him than ever.

There is that vain, worldly, utterly carnal woman. She dresses, speaks, and acts to draw attention to herself, as if all her worth depends on being adored and applauded by others. She is in perpetual competition with all other females; she cannot abide for anyone else to be praised without slipping in a little something about her own successes, showing that she is just a little bit better than others. Perhaps she is a mother proud of her house and its contents but secretly regretting that her family prevents her from really spreading her wings, painfully conscious of all the sacrifices that she has had to make for everyone else. Her children are always more talented, gifted, precocious, and precious than others—they attain more, more quickly and more evidently than others. Or perhaps she is in the world of business, determined to outdo the women and out-man the men, desperate, vulgar, aggressive, full of herself, and deeply dissatisfied, without any sense of what would fill her soul. But then one day she is found happy in her own skin, and not from the latest self-help magazine or because of the latest makeover of her face, family, or home. Rather, she is learning to esteem others more highly than herself, and a spirit of feminine beauty begins to pervade her being. Gentleness, graciousness, and kindness begin to manifest themselves in her life. She still works hard, but the self-defeating spirit of competition has given way to peace, a growing measure of contentment, as if she is measuring herself by a different standard and seeing herself in a different light.

There is that bigoted, self-obsessed, arrogant man. He must always have the last word, must always be noticed. His wife, or the latest of his women, must be what he wants her to be. His home, car, clothes, and children must reflect his authority, power, presence, and salary. No one is allowed too close; no one steps behind the walls of his soul. He absorbs all criticism against himself but dispenses it readily concerning others. He cannot be wrong—he cannot afford to be wrong—for his sense of self and his imagined image in the mind of others would crumble. He cannot be seen to be weak, for he must seem to be strong if he is to maintain his façade of competent control. The world must revolve around him; he must be the sun at the center of every system, and those planets which will not fall into orbit around him will be slung out as dead rocks. His life is a desperate attempt to stay on top of the heap, and his soul is full of bitterness because he believes that he is the only person who truly recognizes his worth. And then one day he asks his wife's opinion. Even more, he actually listens to it. He actually commends one of his colleagues for a good job or encourages one of his employees. He is willing to let his guard down, to begin dismantling the walls that have kept all potential rivals at arm's length. He stops pretending to be what he is not and is learning to be content with what he is.

There is that dry soul locked into religious armor, a mere husk of seeming godliness. This one is always in place, Sunday by Sunday, morning and evening. Perhaps she reads her Bible and says her prayers every day. Her orthodoxy cannot be questioned; she can sniff a heretic at a thousand paces. She is happy for the preacher to speak the truth but believes that the Holy Spirit should be left to do the application. She is very happy to hear hypocrisy addressed and hopes that Mrs. Jones was listening carefully. In her view, sanctification is by vinegar, and she lives her life in the accusative case, very quick to let it be known when things and people have not reached the required standard. She does not particularly want to see those rowdy young people coming into the meetings. They can be heard speaking before the service—and have you seen the state in which they leave the toilets? When the time comes for a new pastor to be appointed, she would like a mature man, one who will not rock the boat, who recognizes that the status quo is the great thing and who can see the worth of the more solid and reliable members of the church—women like herself, for instance. But one day the Word of God hits home, and that woman is seen to feel her sins—to weep over them—for the first time. She forgets the state of the building and even forgets to tut at the noise of the children, so caught up is she with the glory of God in Christ. After a few weeks, she is found chatting with someone about the beauty of the Lord Jesus. Her public prayers among the women, once massive and dull, are now stuttering out of a broken heart, filled with thankfulness to a saving God and an appetite for godliness rather than respectability, with petitions crashing like waves upon the shores of heaven.

We could paint a thousand portraits of misery of greater or lesser inward sorrow and outward rebellion, of spiritual deadness, and then sketching with lines of increasing vibrancy and vigor a picture of genuine life springing into being where before there was nothing.

What has happened? What is happening? "The old has gone and is gone for good; the new has come and keeps on coming." These transformations, step by step, sometimes slow and painful, especially where they are working against patterns of long-ingrained sin, are the result of that sinner being carried out of the kingdom of darkness and translated into the kingdom of the Son of God's love. It might be said that, for the first time, you have found these men and women, boys and girls, clothed and in their right mind. The demons are gone, and peace with God has been established. This is marvelous in our eyes, is it not? Here is one who, after years of living for self and in sin, is now living "for Him who died for me and rose again." It is the same soul, but with utterly different qualities working through it. It is the same body, but now enlivened by an entirely different spirit. This one has new light, new understanding, a new will, new desires and inclinations, new pursuits and purposes, and a new destiny—she is in Christ and will one day be with Christ! In the words of Matthew Henry, "The renewed man acts from new principles, by new rules, with new ends and in new company."[3] To be sure, many of the fruits of grace are—to begin with—in the bud rather than in the bloom, but there is new life flowing through the veins, and the transformation will continue: "Behold, the new has come and keeps on coming!"

Can you hear the note of gospel triumph in Paul's cry, "Behold!"? "Look at this!" he says, holding up the trophy of grace to the wondering gaze of our delighted eyes. Can you not go back with him to a dusty road many years before, where a bitter, bigoted man rode with a heart full of vicious intentions to persecute—utterly to crush and bring to nothing—this perverted sect of the accursed Nazarene? That man was confronted by the one person he never expected to see—the risen Jesus, the glorified Christ in all His majesty and purity, in all the awesome splendor of His person and in all the pomp of His saving accomplishments—and the scales fell from his spiritual eyes even as they closed up his physical ones. This is Saul of Tarsus, able to see Christ and others only according to the flesh, governed by his own carnal convictions and driven by his own pride and bitterness, "a blasphemer, a persecutor, and an insolent man" (1 Tim. 1:13), full of arrogant hatred. He meets Jesus of Nazareth, once crucified, now crowned, and divine grace impels him out of the kingdom of darkness into God's marvelous light: "Behold, all things have become new." Saul of Tarsus sees with new eyes, is governed by new principles, has new aims and desires, is under a new authority, and lives with a new and unshakeable hope: he is a new creation in Christ, and the world will know him soon as the apostle Paul, a little man with a great God and Savior.

Do you have such a "Behold!" in your life? Do not draw the wrong conclusion here. As we will see, the issue is not the outward circumstances of the conversion but the inward reality. The mark of being in Christ is the reality of the new creation, and a person can be born again under a gentle breeze as much as in a thundering

---

3. Matthew Henry, *Matthew Henry's Commentary* (Peabody, Mass.: Hendrickson, 1991), 6:500.

storm. We do not need to undergo the kind of crisis that Saul of Tarsus experienced, but we must experience the same essential transition. In every Christian's life is the evidence that the old has gone and is gone for good, and the wonder that the new has come and keeps on coming. Stage by stage, degree by degree, line upon line, and precept upon precept, the principles and structures of the old life are dismantled and rebuilt to reflect the radical reality of the new man who dwells within.

So if you are a new creation in Christ, as we shall see, God will complete that which He has so gloriously begun! But we need to see and feel, truly to understand and appreciate the incongruity —the utter weirdness and wrongness—of being in Christ and walking in our old ways. Old habits die hard. Old patterns are hard to break. Therefore, the Lord calls us to live as those who have put off the old man and put on the new: "But you have not so learned Christ, if indeed you have heard Him and have been taught by Him, as the truth is in Jesus: that you put off, concerning your former conduct, the old man which grows corrupt according to the deceitful lusts, and be renewed in the spirit of your mind, and that you put on the new man which was created according to God, in true righteousness and holiness" (Eph. 4:20–24).

If you were massively overweight but embraced a particularly effective regime of diet and exercise, resulting in the loss of huge amounts of weight, would you be able to wear the same clothes as before? Of course not! How much more the new man in Christ, a new creation by God's grace, an heir of the death and resurrection of Jesus, whose old man was crucified with Him and who now needs to put off the trappings of the grave and put on, by Christ's power and grace, those accessories becoming a new man, in accordance with the reality of the new creation? When Lazarus came out of the grave, he was bound hand and foot with grave clothes, and his face was wrapped with a cloth. Jesus commanded those around, "Loose him, and let him go" (John 11:44). How much more when we rise to newness of life in Him ought we to be rid of our grave clothes and set free to live as God intends?

But as there is hope for the ongoing, increasing transformation of the child of God, so there is hope for the child of wrath. There is no need to despair, either on our own account or on account of any others. No one but God has ever been able to make a man or woman, boy or girl a new creation, but God can—and God does. This is a work of God's mighty power in which the soul is turned from darkness to light, in which life floods that which once was only dead. There are none so deep in sin, so far from Christ, that they are beyond the reach of God's mighty power and outstretched arm; He, but He alone, can draw them in and draw them up, and this He does through the gospel of His Son, Jesus Christ. Let us not trust in educators, politicians, mystics, medics, moralists, philosophers, spiritualists, and scientists, though some may have their place. The new life in Christ is secured and advanced through the powerful entrance of the gospel, which effectively works in those who believe. Whoever comes to Christ in faith—repenting of his sins, seeing his misery without Christ, seeking grace to be in Christ—and earnestly desiring that one day he might see and be with Christ—will find Christ to be his Savior and Lord and will enter into the blessed realities of the new creation in himself now and look forward to a life in a new heaven and new earth with Christ in days to come, the very heaven of heaven.

For Further Reflection

1. What might be the effects of not accepting or understanding that a Christian is "in Christ"?

2. Without Christ, with Christ, and in Christ. Briefly describe each state, and consider your own present condition and future expectations.

3. Why is it so important that this radical and thorough change is accomplished by divine power? What difference does that make?

4. "The old has gone and is gone for good; the new has come and keeps on coming." Briefly explain the two parts of this declaration.

5. If you profess to be a Christian, what are some of the changes that you have started to see in yourself in keeping with your new nature?

6. What is the effect of being a new creation with regard to the old patterns of sinfulness in a Christian's life?

Chapter 3

THE UNSEARCHABLE
RICHES OF CHRIST

*T*he apostles seem to have existed, at times, in a state of humble wonder. Their admiring cries of "Behold!" echo throughout Scripture as they turn the multifaceted jewel of redemption in the light of God's revelation, entering into the spirit of angelic praise as they endeavor "to comprehend with all the saints what is the width and length and depth and height—to know the love of Christ which passes knowledge" (Eph. 3:18–19).

Paul's sense of his own just deserts and God's undeserved kindnesses implant in him an ever increasing sense of awe at the grace that has made him not only a Christian but also—in his case—a minister of Christ, a preacher of the good news. Paul thinks little of himself, much of others, and most of Christ. He would not dream of preaching himself—he would have nothing to say. He does not preach a *what*, but a *whom*; Paul is taken up with the unsearchable riches of Christ. "Behold Christ!" is his motto. His gospel is Christ in all His saving splendor. It is for this reason and in this spirit that he writes to the Ephesians:

> For this reason I, Paul, the prisoner of Christ Jesus for you Gentiles—if indeed you have heard of the dispensation of the grace of God which was given to me for you, how that by revelation He made known to me the mystery…that the Gentiles should be fellow heirs, of the same body, and partakers of His promise in Christ through the gospel, of which I became a minister according to the gift of the grace of God given to me by the effective working of His power.

To me, who am less than the least of all the saints, this grace was given, that I should preach among the Gentiles the unsearchable riches of Christ." (Eph. 3:1–3, 6–8)

If John Newton had lived and written hymns in Paul's day, the apostle might have readily sung, "Amazing grace! How sweet the sound, that saved a wretch like me!" He is "less than the least of all the saints," and yet he has been sent to make Christ known. Paul never ceased to be amazed by God's grace in Christ Jesus, seeming always to possess in his soul a present sense of his own blessings: made a man of God and a minister of the gospel. Paul used such language and felt the realities that lie behind it.

He is characterized by a sense of awe at the grace of God that he has received in the face of his sin, wickedness, rebellion, and ignorance—all his striving against God. God showed grace in Christ, and so the unsearchable riches of Christ bubble up continually out of the apostle's thankful soul. Christian, is grace still amazing to you? You may not be called to declare these riches in the same way as Paul or other preachers, but you have nevertheless—if you are a child of God—received them, and you ought to know it and enjoy it.

The Glorious Riches Described

Paul describes these riches as indescribable; we are defeated before we begin, but it is at least an honorable defeat. These riches are, says the apostle, without footprint. They are unexplored vistas, a trackless sea so wide that it cannot be measured, so deep that it cannot be plumbed.

Paul makes clear that the revelation of God's goodness in Christ Jesus never destroys wonder—it only creates it. If you think that you have learned enough about Jesus that it is starting to become familiar, then you are not learning Jesus as you should. The more Paul knows, the more he realizes he does not know. The closer he gets, the further away he feels himself to be. The longer he looks, the more he sees; the more he knows, the more he realizes there is to know and the more he appreciates that he can never know all there is to know and can never measure the vastness of the riches to be found in Jesus Christ.

Paul's highest thoughts are too low, his sweetest words too bitter, his deepest insights and expressions too shallow, his broadest view too limited for this task. His faculties are, in that sense, defeated by the unsearchable riches found in Christ as Savior, the revealed truth of the Lord Jesus. And if that is true of a man of such penetrating insight and profundity of thought and breadth of imagination as the apostle, how much more of you and me?

The fact that these riches are unsearchable does not, of course, mean that we should not search them, but it does mean that all our searching will never come to the end of them. Christ is like a palace with countless rooms, each one filled with splendid treasures, each treasure of exquisite worth and beauty, so much so that should we revisit any room we realize that we have not begun to take account of any one of the treasures, let alone the mass of them in that room alone, which is only one of a thousand rooms to explore. We search, confident that there is always more to be found, always more worth finding.

What are some of these riches? We might begin with the unsearchable love of Jesus Christ. Paul delights in this, speaking of how God "chose us in Him before the foundation of the world, that we should be holy and without blame before Him in love" (Eph. 1:4). He roots the intentions and actions of the Father toward us in His abounding love: "But God, who is rich in mercy, because of His great love with which He loved us" (Eph. 2:4). He prays that the saints may come "to know the love of Christ which passes [far exceeds] knowledge; that you may be filled with all the fullness of God" (Eph. 3:19). This is an electing love, a love which chose us when there was nothing in us worth choosing. It is a love vast as the ocean, lovingkindness in full flood. It is a love that comes from One who is utterly holy, who embraces with saving power those who are entirely unholy. It is a love demonstrated in nothing less than the cross of Golgotha, the appalling and agonizing death of the One who loves on behalf of the ones whom He loves. Its greatness is inscribed in the love of the Father in giving the Son, in the love of the Son in giving Himself for those who were still sinners.

But there is also *unsearchable grace* from God in Christ. All salvation is "to the praise of the glory of His grace, by which He made us accepted in the Beloved" (Eph. 1:6). We are made to sit in the heavenlies in Christ in order "that in the ages to come He might show the exceeding riches of His grace in His kindness toward us in Christ Jesus" (Eph. 2:7). Who can plumb the depths of the free favor of God toward the ungodly? This is a grace that crosses the gulf of sin, that bestows the best of blessings upon the most unworthy objects.

There is *unsearchable forgiveness* in Christ: "In Him we have redemption through His blood, the forgiveness of sins, according to the riches of His grace" (Eph. 1:7). Samuel Davies teaches us to sing of

> *Pardon for sins of deepest dye,*
> *A pardon sealed with Jesus' blood.*[1]

In Christ Jesus there is pardon for the worst of sins and sinners, there is blood to make the foulest wretch entirely clean before the searching eye of the God who is "of purer eyes than to behold evil" and who "cannot look on wickedness" (Hab. 1:13).

There is *unsearchable wisdom* in Christ: "In Him we have redemption through His blood, the forgiveness of sins, according to the riches of His grace which He made to abound toward us in all wisdom and prudence" (Eph. 1:7–8). From whichever angle you approach it and whatever perspective you consider it, whether you consider the plan of God's salvation, its execution, its distribution, or our present experience of it, the unsearchable riches of wisdom in Christ are dictating, directing, and dispensing these riches of grace to all people.

Then there is *unsearchable power* in Christ: "having made known to us the mystery of His will, according to His good pleasure which

---

1. Samuel Davies, "Great God of Wonders! All Thy Ways."

He purposed in Himself, that in the dispensation of the fullness of the times He might gather together in one all things in Christ, both which are in heaven and which are on earth—in Him" (Eph. 1:9–10). Here is the revealed truth of God's Word. Here is God's settled purpose: that when history comes to a climax, Jesus Christ will have gathered together in Him all things, both in heaven and on earth. This "is the exceeding greatness of His power toward us who believe, according to the working of His mighty power which He worked in Christ when He raised Him from the dead and seated Him at His right hand in the heavenly places, far above all principality and power and might and dominion, and every name that is named, not only in this age but also in that which is to come" (Eph. 1:19–21). It is the resurrection power that is at work in the believer. It is the power that is going to accomplish all of God's purposes from eternity to eternity, binding together in Christ all whom the Lord intends to bless. Think of the power that is in Christ Jesus, whereby these divine purposes are worked out with an eye on a future so distant that humans cannot begin to comprehend it!

Furthermore, there is *unsearchable joy* in Christ Jesus. "In Him also we have obtained an inheritance, being predestined according to the purpose of Him who works all things according to the counsel of His will, that we who first trusted in Christ should be to the praise of His glory" (Eph. 1:11–12). Those in Christ have the joy of the inheritance of the saints in the light, an eternal and unshakeable kingdom now and to come—the joy, as forgiven sinners, of entering into that world of love for which we are being kept by the power of God.

There is *unsearchable truth* in Christ: "In Him you also trusted, after you heard the word of truth, the gospel of your salvation" (Eph. 1:13). Who, says Paul, can appreciate the wonder of the good news in Christ Jesus? Who has exhausted those precious promises? Who has understood all those shining certainties which are "Yes" and "Amen" in Christ to the glory of God, this revelation of life abundant that Christ has brought in and with Himself (2 Cor. 1:20)? "Oh, the depth of the riches both of the wisdom and knowledge of God! How unsearchable are His judgments and His ways past finding out!" (Rom. 11:33). He is the fountain of life, full of grace and truth.

There is *unsearchable assurance* in Christ. "In Him you also trusted, after you heard the word of truth, the gospel of your salvation; in whom also, having believed, you were sealed with the Holy Spirit of promise, who is the guarantee of our inheritance until the redemption of the purchased possession, to the praise of His glory" (Eph. 1:13–14). This is the powerful work of the Spirit in Christ's people. Where does any Christlikeness come from? Where does any love for God come from? Where does any hope of heaven come from, if not from the Spirit, who is the guarantee of our inheritance? He is the One in whom, possessing Him and possessed by Him, we are stamped with the builder's sign, the owner's mark. The indwelling of the Spirit testifies of God, "These are My work and My people, and what I have begun I will finish."

Therefore, there is *unsearchable hope* in Christ: " the eyes of your understanding being enlightened; that you may know what is the hope of His calling, what are the riches of the glory of His inheritance in the saints" (Eph. 1:18). There is abiding joy because of what is coming, sweet assurance that it will come, and then this sparkling hope, this fixed future of unspeakable glory, the riches of the glory of the inheritance in the saints for every child of God. There is untold goodness still coming to break upon the heads of the children of God!

There is *unsearchable mercy* in Christ: "But God, who is rich in mercy, because of His great love with which He loved us" (Eph. 2:4). This is the mercy which turns rebels from their rebellion, has an ear for the near-despairing cry of the lost, opens its arms to the returning sinner, bestows life on the dead, and gives gifts beyond comparison to the outcast, the mercy of a God who

> *raises the poor from the dust*
> *And lifts the beggar from the ash heap,*
> *To set them among princes*
> *And make them inherit the throne of glory.* (1 Sam. 2:8)

Paul has recorded in scant outline in this letter to the Ephesians only *some* of the unsearchable riches of Christ. He is scratching the surface, picking up a few of the diamonds that lie in the topsoil. He could speak of the riches of Christ's righteousness, compassion, goodness, and on and on. The apostle says that none of them can properly be fathomed. No one has ever walked through these fields, climbed these mountains, traversed these valleys; no one has ever explored these trackless seas to their depths and extents, traced the rushing rivers to their source—the Lord Jesus Christ is in Himself a whole world of wonder! Unsearchable riches, and all of it bathed in glory, limned with divine light. Paul says again and again that all this is to the praise of the glory of His grace. It is all to the praise of God in Christ. God is the Father of glory and Christ the Lord of glory; every line of the revelation of God in Christ is all lit up with the divine majesty.

However much you think you know these things, they remain unexhausted and inexhaustible. You have barely started to know them. They are so vast that you cannot reach the end of them. They are so intricate that no matter how you trace them with the fingers of your most incisive thoughts, no matter how carefully you discern the beauty and wisdom of these works of God, you will never be able to come to the end or be able to put it all together. You must stand back and gaze again at the tapestry of God's saving works through Christ Jesus and say, "These things are beyond searching out. Here I bow, defeated and adoring." If you had a thousand lifetimes, you would need a thousand, thousand more even to begin to understand these things. Only eternity will give you time enough to start searching out more of the unsearchable riches of Christ.

Paul, the other apostles, and those who have followed them have been exploring and proclaiming these unsearchable riches for some two thousand years (and there were those who began to see them gleaming before the incarnation). Two thousand years of sermons have not yet plumbed the deepest depths and marked the highest heights of the riches found in Jesus Christ. They have been searched, they are being searched, they will be searched, and they do prove and will prove unsearchable. But what every saint must grasp—what we long for all people to grasp—is that these unsearchable riches are all found *in Christ*.

The Glorious Person Identified

All this is found in Christ Himself, in Him alone. Notice that they are not simply the unsearchable riches that come from or through Christ. They are the unsearchable riches *of Christ Himself*: "Blessed be the God and Father of our Lord Jesus Christ, who has blessed us with every spiritual blessing in the heavenly places *in Christ*" (Eph. 1:3, emphasis added). When God puts us in Christ He unites us with Christ and all that belongs to Him. These unsearchable riches are those treasures, spiritual blessings in the heavenly places, which are found in Him alone. He Himself is the treasure and the treasury. He Himself is the gift and the giver. The benefits and the benefactor cannot be separated from each other. Here truth is both known and enjoyed. He is the revelation and the repository of all salvation blessings. The streams we drink of flow from and belong to the fountain. Because they are Christ's riches, they are unsearchable. This is what gives them their unfathomable character.

True Deity

This is so because Christ possesses true deity. He is the infinite, unchangeable, and eternal God. These things that are made known in Him and that we experience in knowing Him come to us with all the depth of divinity and height of Godhead. The love that is of Christ is divine love; the forgiveness that is of Christ is divine forgiveness; the grace is divine grace; the wisdom and power are the wisdom and power of the omniscient and omnipotent God, the One who knows and can do all things.

As the Puritan Stephen Charnock discusses the knowledge of God, he reminds us that God knows not just what He has done, but He also knows everything His infinite power could possibly accomplish. Furthermore, everything that His infinite knowledge can grasp lies within His power to carry out if He should wish. God doesn't just know everything we know about perfectly, He knows all that could possibly be known about Himself and all things possible—past, present, and future—and He can do whatever He pleases within the sphere of His knowledge. If He can know it, He can do it; if He can do it, He can know it.[2] There are no limits, no boundaries, no borders in God, and Christ is God. These are divine riches indeed!

True Humanity
But with His true deity is joined true humanity, for it is as the Anointed One that He stands before us. These riches are, in part, unsearchable, because they were wrought on the anvil of His flesh in the workshop of this world, ultimately under the hammer of the cross. If you and I are to begin to understand these things—this love, wisdom, and power—then we must understand them in the God who, because He loved, became man and took upon Himself flesh and blood. This is why we may sing,

> O what matchless condescension
> The eternal God displays,
> Claiming our supreme attention
> To His boundless works and ways.[3]

It is as much in this unfathomable stooping down—the crossing of the immeasurable distance between true Godhead and real humanity, assuming the form of a man, becoming a servant—as in anything else that God shows us the depths, splendor, vastness, and wonder of the riches of Christ Jesus. It is in the God who became man that we know these salvation blessings. The depth of the degradation to which He stooped, the reality of humanity *for us*, demands of us again answers to the questions, "How can I get to the bottom of these things? How can I understand the love

2. Stephen Charnock, *The Existence and Attributes of God*, in *The Works of Stephen Charnock* (Edinburgh: Banner of Truth, 2010), 1:467–69.
3. William Gadsby, "O What Matchless Condescension."

that drove this? How can I grasp the wonder of a forgiveness that is opened by the incarnate Son?"

True Agony

But let us not forget His true agony. This salvation was hammered out with judgment, forged in the furnace of affliction. The jewels of these unsearchable riches were mined in the depths of Christ's sorrows. They were brought up from the darkness of His dereliction on the cross, His isolation from men, and His forsakenness by God: "My God, My God, why have You forsaken Me?" (Matt. 27:46). This is where your salvation was won. When you begin to understand the price that was paid, only then will you begin to understand the blessings bestowed. Who can go as deep as Christ has gone? Who can suffer as intensely as He? Who can understand the price Jesus paid that we should no longer be cast out but brought in? Who can appreciate the agonies of body and soul that this God-man underwent? He bore in His body on the tree all the sufferings that His people deserved, exhausting God's wrath, taking upon Himself the hell that His chosen ones deserved. He bore in His hands and head and side and feet, inscribed with nails and thorns and spears, the names of those He loved, their persons borne on His heart like the high priest of old going into the Most Holy Place. There He goes as our sacrifice and representative. There the fire of God's wrath descends on Him, and the hammer of divine judgment crashes down upon Him, and Christ, in the darkness of that day and of His soul, cries out of the depths of misery that only this Jesus could understand and experience, that He has been forsaken of His Father. Only then does He climb back out of the depths of His sufferings and, before He gives up His spirit, cry out in triumph, "It is finished!"

That is why the riches are unsearchable. When you can walk where Christ walked, you can appreciate the wonders of the salvation blessings to be found in Him. Here we find true deity (He is God) and true humanity (He becomes man) in true agony— suffering to purchase our redemption blessings.

True Glory

And there is true glory, for where does He now sit? Enthroned in the heavenly places at the right hand of God. There is no higher place in which He could sit, and from there He is bestowing these riches upon us. As we cannot plumb the depths from which He mined these precious things, neither can we scale the heights from which they are bestowed. He is the reigning conqueror, waiting until His enemies are made His footstool. It is from there that the Holy Spirit—the foretaste of all that is to come, who gives us the assurance and guarantee of these things—is poured out upon us. There, in the Most Holy Place not made with hands, the people of God have a Great High Priest who is ever living to make intercession for them. There, the flock of God has a Shepherd who shepherds His sheep moment by moment. This same Christ, in all the wonder of His risen glory, ascended up into the highest heaven, is there crafting and sending these gifts of divine and human love, the Messiah's mercies to His chosen people.

You cannot know these blessings apart from Jesus Christ or find them other than in Him. You cannot experience them until you are in Christ. You cannot receive them without Him, because these are the unsearchable riches of Christ, belonging to and found in Him alone. As we have said, He is both treasury and treasure. You cannot open the box, take out the treasures, and walk away with them. They belong in the display cabinet and are splendid in themselves. In the abstract, love, forgiveness, truth, power, hope, and mercy are beautiful and good in themselves and can be great things. But it is when they are found in and of Christ that they are constituted unsearchable, and being of Christ, they are for salvation. To be found in Him is to come into possession of them. Because they belong to Him and are found in Him, they stretch beyond human comprehension. It is because they are of Him and in Him—our Ransomer—that they are given for human blessing.

A Glorious Mystery Proclaimed

The Messiah's riches are for Gentile sinners as well as Jewish
ones. In this letter Paul is both preaching—he is proclaiming
good news—and recording the fact of this preaching among the
Gentiles, the nations of the world. He is preaching to make all see
the fellowship of the "mystery, which from the beginning of the
ages has been hidden in God who created all things through Jesus
Christ" (Eph. 3:8–9).

Why are these things being declared by Paul and those who
stand where he stands and work where he works? Why have they
been made known in Jesus Christ? Are they just to tantalize and
frustrate us? Are they to be regretted and mourned over because
we cannot get them, because they are constantly held just out of
our reach—to be resented because, though they exist, they are kept
from us?

The unsearchable riches of Christ are proclaimed in order that
they might be known and enjoyed, received by sinners who have
come to rest in the boundless resources of Jesus Christ as their
Deliverer, the One given for the very purpose of meeting the needs
of fallen people. That in itself is unsearchable!

> Let the wicked forsake his way,
> And the unrighteous man his thoughts;
> Let him return to the LORD,
> And He will have mercy on him;
> And to our God,
> For He will abundantly pardon.
>
> "For My thoughts are not your thoughts,
> Nor are your ways My ways," says the LORD.
> "For as the heavens are higher than the earth,
> So are My ways higher than your ways,
> And My thoughts than your thoughts." (Isa. 55:7–9)

Salvation is the reason these things are stored up in Jesus
Christ. God's saving purpose provides the only explanation for the
proclamation of the divine treasure and treasury. These riches are

deposited in the incarnate Son so that they might be found and obtained by sinners like us. Everything to save and satisfy the soul is there in the Lord Christ. These unsearchable riches of Christ are good news proclaimed. They constitute in themselves a saving offer to sinners. They are declared to be received. They are not stored up to be kept away but in order that they might be granted in all their fullness, that they might be received, embraced, tasted, and taken in by those who in themselves are utterly foul and needy.

Paul says, in effect, "I cannot tell all to all, but I will tell all I can to all I can. I will declare everything I can search out of these unsearchable riches to the Gentiles into whose presence I come, that I might make them all see what is the fellowship of this mystery, that they too might come into possession of the glorious wealth of Messiah Jesus. These are no limited mercies, no restricted blessings. They no longer belong to any one particular nation or group, but now they are being declared to all the world so that sinners of every kind, from every place, through every time, might themselves come to possess—not just know about but hold fast to—these unsearchable riches that are found in Christ alone."

How utterly ridiculous, then, to look elsewhere for blessing! What misery to pursue good in any other place but in Christ. Will anybody ever find such enduring wonders in the bubbles and baubles of this world? Is there anything you know that can accurately be described like this—unsearchably rich, unfathomably wondrous? How can you compare the dust and ashes of this world with the golden glories of Christ? The best things that this world has to offer—and it does have some legitimately beautiful things—are like the sand of the desert grasped in the clutching hand of a dying man. Most of it runs through our wasting fingers, and—no matter how golden in appearance—the grains that are left are simply sand.

If you clutch solely at the sand of this world you will always be dissatisfied and—what is far worse—you will be lost forever. This is the folly and misery of those who seek their blessings outside of and apart from Christ. But it is also the confusion and error of too many of the saints. How many of us confuse sand and gold dust?

How many of us seek our treasures here or set out to combine gold and sand? How many of us try to keep our hands full of sand while the gold lies within reach?

The world, considered as a source of satisfaction, will always disappoint us. Its best treasures are tainted and passing. Faith looks beyond the offerings of this present life and sets its affections on the things that are above: "By faith Moses, when he became of age, refused to be called the son of Pharaoh's daughter, choosing rather to suffer affliction with the people of God than to enjoy the passing pleasures of sin, esteeming the reproach of Christ greater riches than the treasures in Egypt; for he looked to the reward" (Heb. 11:24–26).

Here is the happiness of those who seek and find their blessing in Christ, who have Him and everything that is in Him. Ours are the spiritual blessings in the heavenlies in Christ. Those riches are unsearchable, but how sweet it is to search them! They are untraceable, but how lovely it is to trace them! They are untrackable, but how delightful it is to track them through the pages of Scripture and experience. They are without footprint, but what a glorious journey of unending exploration! And all of them are stored up in Christ Jesus our Lord. He is the storehouse, and His are the treasures stored within. When you have Him, you have all good things in and with Him. If you have any of them, it is only because you have Him first.

And He is freely offered still. I hope that you have come to know Him, that you have been blessed with possessing the unsearchable riches of Christ. If you do not yet possess them, they are proclaimed to be received and enjoyed by you. Believe that, and believe in Christ in order to receive them. They are not revealed to be regretted or resented but to be seen and known and obtained by sinners. They are declared in order to be grasped, so that sinners like us may live, like Paul, in a perpetual state of humble wonder.

Is that your condition? Has grace become and remained amazing to you? Do you possess in your soul something of a recurring, if not constant, awareness of your own deserving, with a present awareness of God's gracious giving in Christ, that you—a rebel, a sinner, a hell-deserving wretch—have come to possess the unsearchable riches of Christ Jesus our Lord? Is your life, then, marked by the awe of divine generosity, love for the God who has loved us, joy in the God who has blessed us, praise to the glory of His grace, not only in time but for all eternity, when you will be able to trace out more and more and more, time without end, of the untraceable, unsearchable, but substantial and wonderful riches of Jesus Christ?

The saint who fails to lay hold of these things in some measure is bound to live at a low ebb. Until we muse on these things, the fire will not burn. Grasping our new identity as those possessed of this Christ in all His matchless beauty and glory is vital to living in accordance with that new identity. As these things are given to be received, so they are given to be pondered and enjoyed: "For all things are yours: whether Paul or Apollos or Cephas, or the world or life or death, or things present or things to come—all are yours. And you are Christ's, and Christ is God's" (1 Cor. 3:21–23).

For Further Reflection

1. What are some of the unsearchable riches of Christ? Are there any that are particularly precious to you? Why? List any that you wish to add to the list in the chapter.

2. Why is it important for you to understand that these are the unsearchable riches of Christ Himself?

3. Divinity, humanity, agony, and glory point us to the unsearchableness of the riches of Christ. Which of these, if any, most communicates to you the depths and heights of these things?

4. For what purpose has the Lord God stored up unsearchable riches in Jesus Christ? What does this mean for sinners like us?

5. What is it about the passing glories of the world that we find so attractive? How can we combat this?

6. What are the dangers to a Christian of failing to grasp the unsearchable riches of Christ?

Chapter 4

SONS OF GOD

*H*ave you ever had the experience of discovering something that made you catch your breath? Perhaps it was standing on a mountaintop and seeing some splendid view stretching out before you. Maybe it was the view from an aircraft as you crossed some mountain range of sublime beauty. It may have been the first time you held one of your children in your arms. It could have been some story of amazing courage or nearly incomprehensible sacrifice. Whatever it was, that moment was too sweet simply to pass by, that reality—whatever it was—was too awesome, too majestic, too gripping simply to walk on without pause or comment. It demanded that you stop, ponder, and marvel.

But I wonder if you have ever had that experience with God's truth? Has some spiritual reality ever so gripped you that you felt that you had no choice but to pause and wonder?

The apostle John had just such an experience when he spoke of the nature and character of God's people, the fact that everyone saved by grace and brought to live a truly and consistently righteous life is born of God. This truth is recorded in his gospel—"But as many as received Him, to them He gave the right to become children of God, to those who believe in His name: who were born, not of blood, nor of the will of the flesh, nor of the will of man, but of God" (John 1:12–13)—and in his first letter: "Behold what manner of love the Father has bestowed on us, that we should be called children of God!" (1 John 3:1).

Remember that this apostle had seen many wonderful things in his life. He had lived alongside the Christ for three years, testifying that if all the things that Jesus did "were written one by one, I suppose that even the world itself could not contain the books that would be written" (John 21:25). He had watched the Lord Jesus perform countless miracles. He had been on the mountain when the Lord was transfigured, His whole appearance manifesting something of His personal majesty as He spoke with Moses and Elijah about His exodus. This disciple "whom Jesus loved" had laid his head on the chest of His beloved friend as He ate His last earthly meal, testifying of His coming sacrifice (John 13:23). He had watched as the Son of Man was beaten to a near pulp by His enemies and mocked by His own people. John had stood at a Roman cross as the incarnate God died in darkness, committing His mother to the disciple's filial care as if to a brother. He and Peter had sprinted to an empty tomb and looked at the place where the body of Jesus had been lying. He had trembled in a locked room for fear of the Jews and found himself face-to-face with the risen Lord. He had stood on the deck of a boat on the Sea of Galilee, heard a voice from the shore with questions and suggestions, and recognized the speaker as the Lord of life. He had watched as the man with whom he had walked and talked, on whom he had leaned, and whom he had watched die and seen alive again, was lifted bodily from the earth and swallowed up in shining clouds as He went to His heavenly throne, there to sit in majesty until He returned again in glory to take His people to be with Him.

All this John had been privileged to see and experience, yet the fact that God has loved sinners in such a way as to call them His sons still makes him catch his breath, prompting an outburst of wonder in which he wants the people of Christ to share: "Behold what manner of love the Father has bestowed on us, that we should be called children of God!" (1 John 3:1).

John Demands Our Attention

"Behold!" When John mentions being born of God, he cannot simply skate past it. He not only has to stop himself, but he wants others to stop as well, so he calls out to us lest we should miss this. He breaks out with a cry of joyful amazement.

He is calling us to *look with care*. John wants you, believer, to do more than have a quick glance at something of passing interest. He is calling you to consider something, to study it diligently. He wants us to ponder this matter and to be instructed by what we observe.

He wants us also to *look at length*. We should not rapidly pass on from this reality. Once we have seen it, we need to drink it in. Our looking should be like the experience of a desperately thirsty man who comes upon a source of pure water. A sip or two is not enough for him: he must immerse himself in the element and guzzle it down until he is satiated. John wants you to fix your eyes here—and keep them fixed—to contemplate this until it penetrates your soul. He calls you to have this truth sink into your mind and heart, to be always looking and much meditating upon these things.

A man named Samuel Scudder once recorded his experience as a student of Louis Agassiz, the celebrated Swiss ichthyologist (scientist with a fish fascination). In essence, Agassiz shut Scudder up with a fish called a haemulon with simple and sparse instructions to look at it. Interspersed with occasional breaks for interrogation, Scudder continued to observe the fish. Every time he offered a new observation, Agassiz was pleased but not satisfied, sending him back with the same instruction. Scudder records the process:

> "That is good, that is good!" he repeated, "but that is not all; go on." And so for three long days, he placed that fish before my eyes, forbidding me to look at anything else, or to use any artificial aid. "Look, look, look," was his repeated injunction.
>
> This was the best entomological lesson I ever had—a lesson whose influence was extended to the details of every subsequent study; a legacy the professor has left to me, as he

left it to many others, of inestimable value, which we could not buy, with which we cannot part.[1]

By virtue of this intense, almost obsessive process, Agassiz taught Scudder to look. It is such a looking to which the apostle calls the child of God. "Look, look, look"—do not stop looking until you have learned to see, until you have begun to see, until these things are imprinted upon your consciousness in such a way that they will never leave you.

How many Christians are guilty of giving no more than a passing glance at the things to which Scripture calls our most careful attention? How slow we are to learn to look! How careless we can be, so that we lose much of the blessing our heavenly Father has intended for us. Are we fearful that we shall get out of our depth when the Spirit Himself is our teacher and helper? Or could it be, perhaps, that we have become arrogant, quickly confident that we have mastered the deep things of God? John was still astounded by the things to which he calls our attention, and I suggest that if such a man as the apostle feels the urge to call you to stop and look, then it would be the height of foolishness to do anything else.

John Directs Our Attention

Mercifully, the apostle John is a little more gracious than Professor Agassiz. While the Swiss academic told Scudder only to look, the beloved apostle gives us some specific direction: "Behold what manner of love the Father has bestowed on us!"

John's language is used in the Bible on those occasions when someone is called to be surprised at something, to give free rein to a sense of wonder and astonishment. So, for example, we find it in Luke 1:29, after the angel has greeted Mary with the unusual words, "Rejoice, highly favored one, the Lord is with you; blessed are you among women!" Mary was troubled at his saying "and considered

1. Samuel H. Scudder, "In the Laboratory with Agassiz," *Every Saturday: A Journal of Choice Reading* (April 4, 1874), http://grammar.about.com/od/classicessays/a/Look-At-Your-Fish-By-Samuel-H-Scudder.htm.

what manner of greeting this was" (Luke 1:28–29, emphasis added). Something in the rich and distinctive titles the angel bestowed on her gave Mary pause for thought. We see it again later in Luke, when Christ is eating at a Pharisee's table and a woman of scandalous reputation in the city brings in an alabaster flask of fragrant oil, kneels weeping at Christ's feet, washing them with her tears and wiping them with her hair before kissing His feet and anointing them with fragrant oil. "Now when the Pharisee who had invited Him saw this, he spoke to himself, saying, 'This Man, if He were a prophet, would know who and *what manner of* woman this is who is touching Him, for she is a sinner'" (Luke 7:39, emphasis added). Again, there is something so distinctive here that the Pharisee contends that if only Jesus had some grasp of it, He would be astonished. Peter uses the same expression concerning the character of the saints, given the approach of the day of Christ:

> But the day of the Lord will come as a thief in the night, in which the heavens will pass away with a great noise, and the elements will melt with fervent heat; both the earth and the works that are in it will be burned up. Therefore, since all these things will be dissolved, *what manner of* persons ought you to be in holy conduct and godliness, looking for and hastening the coming of the day of God, because of which the heavens will be dissolved, being on fire, and the elements will melt with fervent heat? (2 Peter 3:10–12, emphasis added)

Here again, the emphasis is on the noteworthy, unusual, distinctive character of the thing to which our attention is drawn.

Often this language is employed about something that is considered unearthly. We find the disciples using it when Christ has stilled the winds and the waves: "So the men marveled, saying, '*Who can this be*, that even the winds and the sea obey Him?'" (Matt. 8:27, emphasis added). Although the words are differently translated here, we might put the question this way: "*What manner of* man is this?"

It is this sense of amazement at something of distinctive and unearthly excellence that John wants to communicate. The apostle wants us to feel the wondrous glory of that which he is considering. It is God's love that so grabs his attention, the divine love of the God who is Himself love (1 John 4:8). The ancient world found the anger of the gods reasonably easy to comprehend; in contrast, the modern world insists that "God is love," failing to put that love in the context of His holiness. The church must continue to contend against capricious and cruel notions of godhead and sentimental and spineless depictions of deity, and it is here that John stands.

He emphasizes that this is indeed a love that comes from God the Father, the God who does abiding good to the utterly undeserving, establishing an intimate relation with them in giving, as a gift of love, His own beloved Son. This is a love without measure flowing from the infinite heart of a good and loving God, an ocean without shore, a realm without frontier.

This love is *everlasting and unchangeable*. God "has bestowed" it—it is a permanent gift. So much in this world is thoroughly unreliable. People in the public eye often boast of their great love and lavish thousands upon extravagant efforts to prove it and then we see that love wither or die just as publicly, sometimes in months and even days. Rarely does it take years. In the modern West, such shabby displays train us to dismiss and devalue love and its declarations. But John makes plain that this is an unshakeable affection, a fixed disposition of God toward His people. This love of God is pitch perfect—it knows no variation. In it there is no rising or falling; it is never off-key. It never fades or dies. This love never erodes but is as sure and constant as God Himself. It is a love of a fixed degree. Consider that a Christian is never more or less loved by his God; the underlying disposition of God toward His children never changes. You are not a son one day and relegated to something less the next, for the love that constitutes us sons does not vary. Thus, our status is secure: we are and must always be sons, and we shall be when time ceases and eternity dawns.

Furthermore, this love is *abounding and unlimited*. Again, it must be measured by the breadth and depth of the heart of God, if one is permitted to speak of measuring the infinite. It is a real gift given, not just a gesture made or a concept explained. John does not take a jewel out of a safe, hold it up to our wondering eyes to tantalize us with its beauty, and then return it to store. Rather, he wants us to look at and value the jewel that has been deposited in our hands as our possession. This is not just something held up before us but something bestowed upon us. God does not merely reveal it to us at a distance; His people know it truly and immanently. It is the love by which the God of heaven has reached across the gulf of sin and called us to be sons. Again, it is simply not possible that we should be carried outside or beyond this love. It must be abounding because of how far it reaches to find us and how much it gives to us, who are utterly undeserving. If I love my son, who loves me, it is a relatively small thing. But if I go to a rebel—my enemy who wrongs me, insults me, and hates me—and I make him my son, then this is love indeed, in that it overcomes so much in the one who is loved and makes him so blessed who deserved only to be cursed. How much more, then, when the Holy One of Israel draws to Himself those who by nature are children of wrath and makes them sons of light?

Again, this love is *undeserved and overwhelming.* Although I have stated it already, it deserves to be made doubly clear. It is, brothers and sisters, a *gift*—a matter of grace alone. It is bestowed, not purchased or earned but freely granted. It does not take the rebel and pardon him, leaving him outside the family, still at a distance. It does not even take the rebel and, having pardoned him, make him a servant within the family. A servant may be privileged, but he is not an heir. Besides, even if he were a servant, he would be only a servant. If he lived and served with perfection, it would not change his nature or alter his status. He could never reach the point at which he would deserve to be a son. But God's love takes the rebel and makes him a son and an heir. Who could deserve this? Who could ever be entitled to be a prince of heaven? And yet that is just what John wants to drive home.

John Holds Our Attention

John carries us to the very heart of the wonder, pointing to and explaining the expression of this love. This is no mere theory, a love that envelopes but does not penetrate. Rather, this love has a profound and perpetual effect upon whomever it touches, altering him or her in the most radical fashion imaginable. John's language throws the emphasis on our new status: *"children of God we are called."*

Children of God! Here is a concept familiar from John's writing: "But as many as received Him, to them He gave the right to become children of God, to those who believe in His name: who were born, not of blood, nor of the will of the flesh, nor of the will of man, but of God" (John 1:12–13). As John introduces this idea in the logical progression of his argument, he is obliged to pause: "If you know that He is righteous, you know that everyone who practices righteousness is born of Him" (1 John 2:29). Born of God! We are those born from above! It is like James's language: "Of His own will He brought us forth by the word of truth, that we might be a kind of firstfruits of His creatures" (1:18). Brought forth by God's own will, by this determinative and decided love! We should note that John is not so much speaking here of our title as of our character; it is not simply about our adoption as sons that he speaks but also of our regeneration. To put it a different way, this is not first a comment on our name but on our nature, for the new name is given in answer to the new nature. You could call me a thousand different things—Mr. Rich, Mr. Handsome, Mr. Intelligent—but the mere addition of a label would not change the grim reality! But we *are* children of God; we have become members of the divine family, and we have had communicated to us the divine nature in this degree. We are one with God not because we have become God, or gods. Rather, as those who practice righteousness in our lives, it is manifest that we are one with Him, born of Him, like Him in a small but real and increasing way—"partakers of the divine nature" (2 Peter 1:4). There has been a revolution in our whole humanity, and it has become our nature to do righteousness. Jesus Christ, the only begotten Son of God, came to save us from our sins; the Spirit of God, who is holy, has renewed us and indwelt us; and now we *are* children of God, doing His works, following His will, walking in His ways, showing true and growing godliness.

And to whom has this blessing been given? On whom has this nature been bestowed? "Children of God *we* are called." There is the note of wonder: that God has granted this gift to us. He has bestowed this matchless, transforming love upon *us*, that *we* should be called the children of God. If you wish to put this book down now and leap for joy, feel free! This new nature has been granted to the lost and guilty, to the sinful and miserable. It is granted to those who have forfeited all claim to God's blessings, who—if left to ourselves—would live and would die utterly cut off from God and all His goodness. We are creatures, mere made beings, and yet called children of God. More, and worse, we are sinning creatures—by nature children of wrath, heirs of sin, burdened with guilt, under the curse, characterized by spiritual darkness; by practice, we were all corruption, disobedience, ingratitude, and rebellion. Notice how John puts himself in our company—John the beloved, John the apostle, John the one who was his Lord's closest friend on earth. There are none so privileged, none so holy, none so advanced, that they ought not to fall on their faces at this, that *we* should be called children of God.

But consider also that "children of God we are *called.*" This is not an opinion; this is a fact. God Himself calls us His children. Men may mock and scorn the church of Jesus Christ. Devils may assault and despise the people of the living God. But our Father looks upon us and declares this to be our enduring and unshake-able nature and status. He is not ashamed to call us children any more than Christ is ashamed to own us as His brothers:

> For both He who sanctifies and those who are being sancti-fied are all of one, for which reason He is not ashamed to call them brethren, saying: "I will declare Your name to My brethren; in the midst of the assembly I will sing praise to You." And again: "I will put My trust in Him." And again:

"Here am I and the children whom God has given Me."
(Heb. 2:11–13)

God publicly acknowledges us as His own in open and
unashamed recognition of this truth. John wants us to feel the
honor of such a title, the high rank and the high responsibility that
goes with it. The Redeemer was not ashamed to make common
cause with us, to take our nature upon Himself and save us by His
death; the Spirit is not ashamed to dwell within us and work upon
us, renewing us and transforming us; the Father is not ashamed to
love us and to call us His children.

John was not outwardly extravagant the way Peter was. When
those men were fishing at dawn on the Sea of Galilee, it was John
who first recognized the risen Christ. His earnest heart drove the
words of adoration from his lips: "It is the Lord!" The fact that it
was Peter who flung himself overboard in order to reach Christ
first should not make us imagine that John's heart beat any less
with love to God.

That is why as soon as he says, "you know that everyone
who practices righteousness is born of Him," he cannot help but
pause and worship: "Behold what manner of love the Father has
bestowed on us, that we should be called children of God! Therefore the world does not know us, because it did not know Him"
(1 John 2:29–3:1).

Let us behold this for *wonder and encouragement.* That sinful
wretches should be constituted and called children of God, prac-
ticing righteousness as those who are born of God, born of the
Spirit, born from above, ought to be something upon which we
fix our eye and our heart, to know and to delight in the goodness
of God toward us. It is a marvel of grace that ought never to cease
to astound us, quite apart from any thankfulness toward the God
who has done it. By this I mean that even if we had no personal
interest in such a declaration, it would be a thing most marvelous
in itself and would reveal something of the heart of God that would
not have been known to mankind without it. That we consider it as

those who have that nature and name bestowed upon us ought not only to make us wonder but also to make us worship.

Let us, furthermore, behold it for *trust and confidence.* The certainty of the saints with regard to these things lies primarily in this, that God has said it. John speaks truth to our hearts: "we are called children of God" as those in whom a new nature reigns. This is not the judgment of man, nor is it merely some subjective sense. It is the declared truth of God in accordance with objective realities. Those who find within themselves an instinct and capacity for righteousness that they did not possess before must conclude that only God could have put it there. How often we are crippled by doubts and fears in this matter: Who am I? What am I? How does God see me? What is His relationship to me? Everyone who does righteousness is born of God. Therefore, you who do righteousness, be sure that this is the love that has been bestowed upon you, that you should be called a son of God by God Himself. Let this be the ground of your assurance.

Behold it, too, for *obedience and fortitude.* This is a truth to hold up the sinking saint under trials and persecutions. "The world does not know us because it did not know Him." This explains the world's reaction to true, vigorous, and decided Christianity: God came into the world, and He was despised and rejected. If we are children of God, having His nature and bearing His name, then we shall suffer the same. The principle holds good that "a disciple is not above his teacher, nor a servant above his master" (Matt. 10:24), as our Lord expounded it before his death:

> If the world hates you, you know that it hated Me before it hated you. If you were of the world, the world would love its own. Yet because you are not of the world, but I chose you out of the world, therefore the world hates you. Remember the word that I said to you, "A servant is not greater than his master." If they persecuted Me, they will also persecute you. If they kept My word, they will keep yours also. (John 15:18–20)

We do well to reckon with this and the reason behind it, for our convictions and comforts with regard to being sons of God will steel us to live to the praise of His glory in the face of such things. God has not been ashamed to call us sons. How, then, can we be ashamed to own Him as our Father and God? We are crown princes of heaven. Why should we live as if we were slaves of sin? To grasp your nature and your name in this atmosphere of love is to grasp your calling and character in this world; this is one of the roots of striving against sin and standing in the midst of sorrows and sufferings. If you are to live as you are called, you must know what you are called.

Behold it for *joy and thankfulness.* Believer, have you grasped this: born of God! You will say—and rightly—that you have not grasped it fully, but have you grasped it really? Have you stopped to consider your new nature and name? If you have not dwelt upon this before, then pause now like a student with some marvel of nature before you: "Look, look, look!" Look until you have begun to grasp something of this incomparable act of a gracious God; look until you have begun to trace out something of the countless excellencies of this gift; look until the broad sweep and the minute details of the beauties of God's mercy begin to come into focus; look until your heart burns within you, and you fall on your face before the Most High God, asking,

> *Why was I made to hear Thy voice,*
> *And enter while there's room,*
> *When thousands make a wretched choice,*
> *And rather starve than come?*

> *'Twas the same love that spread the feast*
> *That sweetly drew us in;*
> *Else we had still refused to taste,*
> *And perished in our sin.*[2]

---

2. Isaac Watts, "How Sweet and Aweful Is the Place."

Have you considered that—flying in the face of all your nature and practice—God Most High loved you with a redeeming and transforming love, a love demonstrated in nothing less than the giving of His only begotten Son that you might be called a son of God? And now, even in the face of all your slipping and stumbling, all your confusion and cold-heartedness, He is not ashamed to own you as one of His children. The relationship is changed entirely: God has given you a new nature, He has bestowed on you a new name, and now you no longer come before God as an enemy but as a child. Think of it, especially if you are a Christian parent: whatever your child may have done, whatever trouble he or she may be in, that child is your child, and you love that child at a deep level with a fierce and tender love which nothing will undo. How much more the Father's love for His children? This should make us weep and shout for joy. Let us, therefore, halt here with John and say with the poet:

> *Pause, my soul, adore and wonder!*
> *Ask, O why such love to me?*
> *Grace hath put me in the number*
> *Of the Saviour's family;*
> *Hallelujah! Hallelujah!*
> *Thanks, eternal thanks, to Thee.*[3]

Finally, we should behold it for *hope*. We have been lost but are found. Many are still wandering but are ripe for the finding. He has made us—and many like us—His children; He has made us—and many at least as bad as us—His saints. He has taken many wolves and goats and made them sheep, many rebels and made them sons, many blasphemers and made them worshipers, many ungodly and made them godly, many who practiced unrighteousness who now practice righteousness as those who are born of God. If He has done it for us, then for whom can He not do it? This is our hope for ourselves and for all the world.

---

3. James George Deck and anonymous, "Father, 'Twas Thy Love That Knew Us."

For Further Reflection

1. In one sentence define or describe one of the truths that makes the apostle John catch his breath in wonder.

2. What sort of looking does John call us to, and why is it important?

3. What, specifically, does John want us to consider in this way, and what are its qualities?

4. What are some of the particular features of God's blessing to which John is calling our attention?

5. Who makes the declaration that we are sons of God, and why is that important?

6. What effects does this declaration have on you? What effects should it have? How do believers and unbelievers differ in this?

Chapter 5

THE JEWEL OF ASSURANCE

The apostle John was a truly pastoral and deeply practical man of God who mixed plainness and profundity like almost no other inspired author. These qualities shine in all his writings. In his gospel as well as in his first and longest letter, he states his intentions in writing. In John 20:31 he tells us that his records of Christ's works and signs "are written that you may believe that Jesus is the Christ, the Son of God, and that believing you may have life in His name." In other words, the gospel of John is primarily an evangelistic production intended, under God, to promote faith and secure conversion. In similar fashion, in 1 John 5:13 John tells us the purpose of his first letter: "These things I have written to you who believe in the name of the Son of God, that you may know that you have eternal life, and that you may continue to believe in the name of the Son of God." It is primarily a pastoral production intended, under God, to promote discernment and secure assurance, and in the next chapter we will go on to look more closely at how John pursues that end.

That You May Know
But we must begin at the right place. If I asked every reader of this book directly, "Are you a Christian?" I would probably get a range of answers. Some might say, "Yes, I am utterly persuaded of it." Others might say, "There is no chance." We must reckon with the possibility of giving either a yes or no answer and being right or

wrong. As you read that last sentence, given starkly and without explanation, you might immediately conclude, "See! It is impossible to know!" Yet if others were asked if they were Christians, they might say, "Oh, I hope so!"—desperate for some way of knowing one way or the other.

Whatever your instinctive or thoughtful response, please consider this: John writes "that you may know." He writes to equip us to answer that question rightly, accurately, legitimately, and properly, and he will provide us with a framework by means of which to examine ourselves in the light of this question.

Assurance Is Definable

Consider first that assurance is *definable*. John says, in effect, that assurance is the knowledge, in those who believe, that they have eternal life. Immediately we should recognize that faith and assurance are related but not identical. All Christians have faith—they believe in the name of the Son of God—but not all Christians are always and fully persuaded of their own salvation. They do not always enjoy the settled conviction that they have eternal life.

Nevertheless, John is making plain that true assurance of salvation belongs to those who believe, and not to those who do not believe. Assurance grows out of the root of faith but is not identical with it. Faith belongs to the essence of salvation, but assurance is part of the health of those who have been saved. To lack assurance of salvation is not the same as lacking the faith that saves through Christ or the salvation that comes through faith. It follows, as we shall see, that if we desire assurance we must first believe, for nothing is more dangerous than the conviction that we are saved without the faith that looks to Christ in order to be saved.

This knowledge that we have eternal life is a present, personal, well-grounded confidence. It is not a guess or a possibility or a mere wish. It is the knowledge of now possessing eternal life, of having been granted as our present and perpetual possession the life that belongs to the risen Lord, the life of the age to come that is begun and enjoyed in this present age. Assurance knows that it has the bud of grace which shall one day bloom fully in glory.

In short, assurance is the well-grounded conviction of true believers that they are in possession of everlasting life, a conviction that rests on faith but is distinct from it and not always present with it. The theologian John Murray defines it in this way: "When we speak of the assurance of faith we mean the assurance entertained by a believer that he is in a state of grace and salvation, the knowledge that he has been saved, has passed from death unto life, has become a possessor of eternal life and is an heir of glory."[1] Thomas Brooks, one of the Puritans, says that "assurance is a reflex act of a gracious soul, whereby he clearly and evidently sees himself in a gracious, blessed, and happy state; it is a sensible [able to be perceived by our senses] feeling, and an experimental [grounded in our experience and able to be tested] discerning of a man's being in a state of grace, and of his having a right to the crown of glory."[2]

Assurance Is Desirable

I hope that such definitions make us testify that assurance of salvation is desirable. While the Bible has its clear warnings against presumption, it nowhere discourages believers from desiring, pursuing, or obtaining a well-grounded assurance of salvation. Sometimes we may be given the impression that there is something noble about uncertainty, something humble about doubt. What is noble about resisting or neglecting God's offered blessings? What is humble about disbelieving God's promises or denying His intentions? Certainty and humility are not mutually exclusive; confidence and presumption are very different things. Just because a good thing can be abused or perverted does not mean that it is bad in itself. David asked the Lord, "Say to my soul, 'I am your salvation'"

---

1. John Murray, "The Assurance of Faith," in *Collected Writings of John Murray* (Edinburgh: Banner of Truth, 1977), 2:264.

2. Thomas Brooks, "Preface: Touching the Nature of Assurance," to *Heaven on Earth*, in *The Works of Thomas Brooks* (Edinburgh: Banner of Truth, 1980), 2:316.

(Ps. 35:3) and was not rebuked or denied, nor did the Lord insist that he retract his request. John desires the assurance of his readers. Was the apostle wrong at this point? Will we deny John's inspiration here? Of course not! John is concerned with regard to assurance because it is a blessing to which every saint—"you who believe" without exception—may attain.

Indeed, if you have a few moments, read the whole of John's first letter. The whole of the New Testament, not to mention the Old, assumes that the saints can, should, and do know themselves to be saints, saved and kept by grace.

Would a husband want his wife to be perpetually unsure of his love for her? Why then should the Lord delight in our doubt, gloom, and uncertainty? As Brooks says, "It is the very drift and design of the whole Scripture, to bring souls first to an acquaintance with Christ, and then to an acceptance of Christ, and then to build them up in a sweet assurance of their actual interest in Christ."[3] So consider briefly just the following passages in demonstration of Brooks's assertion. Peter speaks of "exceedingly great and precious promises" given to us,

> that through these you may be partakers of the divine nature, having escaped the corruption that is in the world through lust.
>
> But also for this very reason, giving all diligence, add to your faith virtue, to virtue knowledge, to knowledge self-control, to self-control perseverance, to perseverance godliness, to godliness brotherly kindness, and to brotherly kindness love. For if these things are yours and abound, you will be neither barren nor unfruitful in the knowledge of our Lord Jesus Christ. For he who lacks these things is shortsighted, even to blindness, and has forgotten that he was cleansed from his old sins.
>
> Therefore, brethren, be even more diligent to make your call and election sure, for if you do these things you will never stumble; for so an entrance will be supplied to you abundantly

---

3. Brooks, "Nature of Assurance," 2:319.

into the everlasting kingdom of our Lord and Savior Jesus Christ. (2 Peter 1:4–11)

The writer to the Hebrews says:

And we desire that each one of you show the same diligence to the full assurance of hope until the end, that you do not become sluggish, but imitate those who through faith and patience inherit the promises....

Thus God, determining to show more abundantly to the heirs of promise the immutability of His counsel, confirmed it by an oath, that by two immutable things, in which it is impossible for God to lie, we might have strong consolation, who have fled for refuge to lay hold of the hope set before us.

This hope we have as an anchor of the soul, both sure and steadfast, and which enters the Presence behind the veil, where the forerunner has entered for us, even Jesus, having become High Priest forever according to the order of Melchizedek. (Heb. 6:11–12, 17–20)

The apostle Paul sows the same expectations and convictions throughout his writings:

For you did not receive the spirit of bondage again to fear, but you received the Spirit of adoption by whom we cry out, "Abba, Father." The Spirit Himself bears witness with our spirit that we are children of God....

Who shall separate us from the love of Christ? Shall tribulation, or distress, or persecution, or famine, or nakedness, or peril, or sword? As it is written: "For Your sake we are killed all day long; we are accounted as sheep for the slaughter." Yet in all these things we are more than conquerors through Him who loved us. For I am persuaded that neither death nor life, nor angels nor principalities nor powers, nor things present nor things to come, nor height nor depth, nor any other created thing, shall be able to separate us from the love of God which is in Christ Jesus our Lord. (Rom. 8:15–16, 35–39)

Now He who establishes us with you in Christ and has anointed us is God, who also has sealed us and given us the Spirit in our hearts as a guarantee. (2 Cor. 1:21–22)

Examine yourselves as to whether you are in the faith. Test yourselves. Do you not know yourselves, that Jesus Christ is in you?—unless indeed you are disqualified. But I trust that you will know that we are not disqualified. (2 Cor. 13:5–6)

In Him you also trusted, after you heard the word of truth, the gospel of your salvation; in whom also, having believed, you were sealed with the Holy Spirit of promise, who is the guarantee of our inheritance until the redemption of the purchased possession, to the praise of His glory. (Eph. 1:13–14)

Therefore do not be ashamed of the testimony of our Lord, nor of me His prisoner, but share with me in the sufferings for the gospel according to the power of God, who has saved us and called us with a holy calling, not according to our works, but according to His own purpose and grace which was given to us in Christ Jesus before time began, but has now been revealed by the appearing of our Savior Jesus Christ, who has abolished death and brought life and immortality to light through the gospel, to which I was appointed a preacher, an apostle, and a teacher of the Gentiles. For this reason I also suffer these things; nevertheless I am not ashamed, for I know whom I have believed and am persuaded that He is able to keep what I have committed to Him until that Day. (2 Tim. 1:8–12)

So why should John be bothered by this matter of assurance? Why am I bothering to write about it? More importantly, why has God so bothered with it as to weave it into the very fabric of His revelation?

It is desirable because an assured believer is a comforted believer. Lack of assurance does not rob a saint of his life but rather of his peace and joy in having life. Assurance will take away those crippling doubts and crushing fears which hinder the saints. It settles the most important question a person will ever ask. With a well-grounded assurance, the child of God knows his journey—however hard and stormy—is going to bring him happily into a safe harbor, enabling him to say with David, "My flesh and my heart fail; but God is the strength of my heart and my portion forever" (Ps. 73:26); and with Habakkuk,

> *Though the fig tree may not blossom,*
> *Nor fruit be on the vines;*
> *Though the labor of the olive may fail,*
> *And the fields yield no food;*
> *Though the flock may be cut off from the fold,*
> *And there be no herd in the stalls—*
> *Yet I will rejoice in the LORD,*
> *I will joy in the God of my salvation.* (Hab. 3:17–18)

Assurance gives strong consolation in sufferings, trials, and even in death.

The assured believer is also a convinced and courageous believer. When we do not know where we stand, we do not know how to act. To know who we are helps us to follow a right course without quibbling or caviling. Am I a child of God? If so, I should live like one! We stop halting between two opinions. We know whose side we are on, and therefore we know who we should fight and how. The assured saint stands before and pleads boldly with God in Christ and then stands boldly before men for God.

The assured Christian ought also to be an active Christian. Assurance is truly liberating for the saint, for in a right measure it turns our attention away from ourselves and our own standing and allows us to direct that energy to service. A settled sense of blessing and privilege breeds a thankful, willing heart. Joy and peace in believing give rise to sacrificial zeal in serving. The fears that cripple others cease to hold back the solid saint; he speaks and serves freely, firmly, positively, and earnestly.

Again, assurance makes a person an advancing Christian. Genuine assurance of salvation never cuts the nerve of holiness. Closeness to God in Christ, communion with the Holy Spirit, assurance of God's love, and awareness of our heavenly hope all tend toward purity of life: "Beloved, now we are children of God; and it has not yet been revealed what we shall be, but we know that when He is revealed, we shall be like Him, for we shall see Him as He is. And everyone who has this hope in Him purifies himself, just as He is pure" (1 John 3:2–3). Such a believer knows his privileges and has a holy horror of abusing them. He hates the thought of offending a reconciled, redeeming God. These people are able to say, "All my springs are in you" (Ps. 87:7) and so find refreshment for their duties and opportunities.

Such blessings should make every child of God not only delight in salvation but also desire the assurance of it. If John writes of assurance in this way, then it is our duty and privilege to pursue it. Here we should cooperate with the apostle; indeed, here we must cooperate with the Spirit of adoption in His intention in revelation and regeneration. Let us not be ashamed to desire it or embarrassed to pursue it.

Assurance Is Possible

Let us not be ashamed to attain it, either, for assurance of salvation is possible. John is not teasing us. The Holy Spirit is not tantalizing us with desirable impossibilities. Why should a living people not know that they are alive? This is not to say that assurance is a thing that necessarily drops into our laps; there are genuine obstacles in the way to attaining and maintaining the assurance of salvation. We must contend with the assaults of Satan, who loves to keep saints in a sad, doubting, troubled, and confused condition. There are misunderstandings to be corrected and false teachings to be avoided; a lack of instruction can hinder us here, as can taking truths such as those concerning election out of context and without scriptural emphasis and proportion. For some, their experience of saving grace is of a more gradual progress, and discerning that progress from one point to the next can be more difficult. Indulging in remaining sin, neglecting known duties, and clinging to the world all undermine our sense of our salvation. For some it is because they are looking in the wrong place or making assessments by the wrong standard. For others, sadly, it may be an unhealthy and unbalanced obsession with assurance which leads to a neglect of those first things upon which assurance is, in fact, established. In addition, but on a different level, we must acknowledge that our heavenly Father, for right and proper reasons (though not discernible to us), may for a period withhold assurance from some of His children.

Even so, it is possible to speak in legitimate tones of settled conviction with regard to this matter. Job could say with relief,

> *For I know that my Redeemer lives,*
> *And He shall stand at last on the earth;*
> *And after my skin is destroyed, this I know,*
> *That in my flesh I shall see God,*
> *Whom I shall see for myself,*
> *And my eyes shall behold, and not another.*
> *How my heart yearns within me!* (19:25–27)

David could say with confidence,

> *The LORD is my shepherd;*
> *I shall not want.*
> *He makes me to lie down in green pastures;*
> *He leads me beside the still waters.*
> *He restores my soul;*
> *He leads me in the paths of righteousness*
> *For His name's sake.*
>
> *Yea, though I walk through the valley*
>   *of the shadow of death,*
> *I will fear no evil;*
> *For You are with me;*
> *Your rod and Your staff, they comfort me.* (Ps. 23:1–4)

Paul could testify, "For I am persuaded that neither death nor life, nor angels nor principalities nor powers, nor things present nor things to come, nor height nor depth, nor any other created thing, shall be able to separate us from the love of God which is in Christ Jesus our Lord" (Rom. 8:38–39); and, "For we know that if our earthly house, this tent, is destroyed, we have a building from God, a house not made with hands, eternal in the heavens" (2 Cor. 5:1); and again, "For this reason I also suffer these things; nevertheless I am not ashamed, for I know whom I have believed and am persuaded that He is able to keep what I have committed to Him until that Day" (2 Tim. 1:12). The writer to the Hebrews calls us to "draw near with a true heart in full assurance of faith, having our hearts sprinkled from an evil conscience and our bodies washed with pure water" (Heb. 10:22). John speaks with confidence: "We know that we have passed from death to life, because we love the brethren" (1 John 3:14); and again, "We know that we are of God, and the whole world lies under the sway of the wicked one. And we know that the Son of God has come and has given us an understanding, that we may know Him who is true; and we are in Him who is true, in His Son Jesus Christ. This is the true God and eternal life" (1 John 5:19–20). We have seen the apostolic intention, and now we see the fruit in the lives of the apostles themselves, and— by extension—in those who, with the blessing of God, receive that intention and pursue its outworking: men and women testifying without bombast or fear of a right standing with God in Christ.

Note that this is not a matter of direct revelation, of voices from heaven whispering into your ear, nor is it necessarily a matter of distinctive, let alone spectacular, experiences of the overwhelming love of God. The 1677/1689 (Second London) Baptist Confession of Faith says that this is found "in the right use of [ordinary] means," under the influence of the Holy Spirit (chapter 18, paragraph 3). Scripture speaks of the Spirit of God being given to us as a guarantee, a divine down payment, and of His enabling us to cry out, "Abba, Father" (Rom. 8:15–16; Gal. 4:6). To complete our earlier quotation from Thomas Brooks:

> Now assurance is a reflex act of a gracious soul, whereby he clearly and evidently sees himself in a gracious, blessed, and happy state; it is a sensible feeling, and an experimental discerning of a man's being in a state of grace, and of his having a right to the crown of glory; and this rises from the seeing in himself the special, peculiar, and distinguishing graces of

Christ, in the light of the Spirit of Christ, or from the testimony and report of the Spirit of God.[4]

It is the Spirit of adoption who works in us faith and its fruits, implanting and stimulating graces which are the evidence of new life and witnessing with our spirit to their presence and reality and owning us by His sweet influences and by these means as children of God. The good grounds of confidence in the life of a saved person produce, through the Spirit's witness, their full effect in our minds and hearts.[5] He is the One who validates those indications of genuine spiritual life which John identifies in his letter. Faith, then, is the foundation, and assurance is the beautiful superstructure, both being the craftsmanship of God by His Spirit. Let us ask Him to do this work and to make it known in His saints.

---

4. Brooks, "Nature of Assurance," 2:316.

5. The sense of this is taken from B. B. Warfield, *Faith and Life* (Edinburgh: Banner of Truth, 1974), 191–92.

For Further Reflection

1. How do you answer the question, "Are you a Christian?" How, then, do you respond to the fact that John writes in order that you may know this clearly and finally?

2. Define "assurance of salvation."

3. Why should assurance be desirable? Is it desirable to you?

4. What are some of the hindrances and difficulties in obtaining assurance of salvation?

5. Do you ever struggle with a lack of assurance? Why?

6. If the Spirit of God is the ultimate architect of assurance, should we and do we ever ask the Lord to give assurance to us or maintain assurance in us?

Chapter 6

THE MARKS OF GOD'S CHILDREN

*B*ecause this matter is so significant, we must now go on to ask what these indications of spiritual life are. What does the foundation look like, and of what is this superstructure constructed? We must go carefully here, because many try to build the house of assurance with materials never intended to supply load-bearing beams. These things are not necessarily worthless or pointless in themselves, but they will not sustain the weight that is put on them if we think to rest our assurance upon them. In other words, people presume upon many things that do not, in themselves, indicate that a work of saving grace has taken place. The world and many outwardly religious people in the world assume many things are certain marks of true Christianity. These things fool many into imagining that they are true believers when they are not. Even many true Christians build their assurance on these things and find that they fail them because they provide no sure foundation. In themselves, they are things which do not allow us to judge whether a profession of faith is genuine or spurious. Their presence or absence does not fully or finally answer the question of whether the person possesses life eternal. They are not "necessary signs"; their presence should not fool us if we are deceiving ourselves, and their absence—properly considered—should not lead us to abandon all hope.

We need to expose and test these things. When that happens, some will find their house of assurance come crashing down around their ears, or—at the very least—begin to creak and shake.

Again, if this leads us to ensure that we have the right foundation and the appropriate materials for the future, this will not harm us but will prosper our souls in the long term. So let us consider some of those things which are not, in themselves, indispensable indications of everlasting life.[1]

Inconclusive Indications

Visible Morality

The first inconclusive indication is visible morality. In 1 Samuel 16:7 the Lord issues Samuel a warning when he is searching for the Lord's anointed: "Man looks at the outward appearance, but the LORD looks at the heart." In the West we may be inclined to look at someone possessed of self-control and not given to riotous excess; who does not sleep around; who has a pleasant, polite, winning personality and—especially in a culture where such behavior is rare—conclude that saving grace is in operation.

It is a great mercy to see such uprightness and restraint in society, and we are not saying that a Christian should have no regard for morality. Indeed, of all people, a Christian ought to be marked by righteousness (Matt. 5:20). But while a Christian *should* be outwardly moral, he *must* be inwardly holy, and those are not necessarily the same thing. An outwardly upright character is no sure indication of love to God. A fair appearance does not necessarily indicate true heart righteousness. The Pharisees were in many respects moral people: they had a shell of external righteousness. When the rich young ruler pointed out his law-abiding life, Christ pressed home the demand of a heart taken up with God rather than the world (Matt. 19:16–22). Moral virtues can exist without gospel graces; you can appear

---

1. The list that follows is from an older work called *The Distinguishing Traits of Christian Character* by Gardiner Spring. This work stands in a stream of longer works, being a condensation of the principles found in such treatments as Archibald Alexander's *Thoughts on Religious Experience* or the Jonathan Edwards classic, *The Religious Affections*, to which you might turn for a more complete assessment of these matters.

creditable outwardly among other people and be despicable inwardly before God. Many people can maintain the façade of morality without ever possessing eternal life and developing true conformity to Jesus Christ. Uprightness of character that does not spring from love to God through a right relationship with Him in Christ, a behavior which has no root in heart holiness, will leave you damned.

Head Knowledge

Another inconclusive indication is head knowledge (mere speculative knowledge or intellectual perception) as opposed to spiritual understanding of the truth. It is possible to know a great deal about Christ without truly knowing Christ; a person can know a lot of the Bible without ever bowing to the God of the Bible (John 5:39). You might know about true religion and have an orthodox creed but have no heart religion (Rom. 1:21). You might have a real intellectual curiosity and a measure of accuracy of perception, but it is possible to possess this speculative knowledge without moving on to spiritual knowledge. Jonathan Edwards emphasized the difference in this way:

> An increase in speculative knowledge in divinity is not what is so much needed by our people as something else. Men may abound in this sort of light, and have no heat. How much there has been of this sort of knowledge, in the Christian world, in this age! Was there ever an age wherein strength and penetration of reason, extent of learning, exactness of distinction, correctness of style, and clearness of expression, did so abound? And yet, was there ever an age, where there has been so little sense of the evil of sin, so little love to God, heavenly-mindedness, and holiness of life, among the professors of the true religion? Our people do not so much need to have their heads stored as to have their hearts touched, and they stand in the greatest need of that sort of preaching which has the tendency to do this.[2]

2. Jonathan Edwards, as quoted in *Jonathan Edwards*, by Iain Murray (Edinburgh: Banner of Truth, 1987), 126–27.

The Pharisees were well instructed (Rom. 2:17–20). The devils have a highly orthodox theology (James 2:19). It is possible to know your Bible inside out, recite the catechism by heart, win Sunday school prizes, excel in theological examinations, receive postgraduate degrees in theology, write books on abstruse theological topics, and to go to hell if that knowledge is not spiritually apprehended (1 Cor. 2:14). Knowledge that produces no movement of the heart or the will toward God is empty. The mere amount you know is no sure register of your state.

Form of Religion

A further inconclusive mark is the form of religion. Many have the appearance of religion without the reality, the form without the power (2 Tim. 3:5). The Pharisees are the prime example of such people, with Jesus in Matthew 23 making one great list of charges against their great reputation for religion combined with a heart far from God. Like many before them and since, their hearts and their mouths told different tales (Isa. 58:2–3; cf. Matt. 15:8). A religion that belongs only to upbringing, operates by a sense of shame, or consists in going with the flow is not a saving religion but a glossy shell. In Matthew 25:1–12 the difference between the two groups of virgins awaiting the bridegroom is the oil; all the outward motions and expectations are the same.

Eminent Gifts

Eminent gifts are another untrustworthy indicator. You may know someone who is good looking, intelligent, sparky, and successful—all seemingly with little or no effort. Does this make him truly good? Of course not, and it is the same in the religious sphere. Some have great natural abilities—sparkling charisma, penetrating intellect, compelling speech. Some possess unusual verbal dexterity—the gift of the gab—but we must remember that John Bunyan became "a great talker in religion" long before he became a true believer. Even Saul was found among the prophets (1 Sam. 10:11–12) and Judas among the apostles (John 17:12). Balaam spoke words full of truth but had a heart full of sin (Num. 22:38). There may be a seeming blessing in the exercise of gifts where there is no real exercise of grace (Matt. 7:22–23).

Conviction for Sin

Treading carefully, we confess that conviction for sin does not resolve the matter. Note that conviction for sin in some measure is *generally necessary for* salvation but *not necessarily joined with* salvation. A person may have a genuine awareness of sin and a real sense of guilt without being converted. Preachers might have seen people weep through a sermon as the truth ploughed up their conscience and then watch as those same individuals walk away and go back to their sin. They were conscious of sin but did not repent of it. Consider that hell is full of people who know themselves sinners; on the day of judgment, many will be persuaded of their sin without being saved. People may deeply feel their sins, profoundly regret their sins, partially forsake their sins, and yet never cease to love their sins. Saul (1 Sam. 26:21), Ahab (1 Kings 21:27–29), Judas (Matt. 27:3), and Felix (Acts 24:25) tell us that conviction need not indicate conversion.

Strong Assurance

Curiously, strong assurance is in itself no sure sign of true conversion. There are many people who are entirely confident that they are on their way to heaven even as they blithely walk the road to hell. What a difference there is between being well and feeling well! The degree of confidence is not the issue. The matter is one of quality rather than quantity, for there is a great difference between believing you are saved and believing in Christ and therefore being saved. Some are utterly blind; some are self-deluded; some are defiantly ignorant. It is possible for someone entirely persuaded that he is right with God to be wrongly persuaded (Matt. 3:7–9); the sense of assurance and the fact of salvation are not the same thing.

Profession of Faith

Again, a notable time or manner of a person's professed conversion is not conclusive. Even unusual and distinctive experiences do not demonstrate that one's profession of faith is genuine. There are some who live and die trusting in the memory of a moment: a holy hot flush, a warm sensation or fuzzy feeling, raising a hand, walking an aisle, responding to an altar call, standing in a gloomy building and being struck with a shaft of sunlight, some sensation of peace, a sense of the numinous in a religious environment.... The list could go on, but all this is possible without a person having known true spiritual life. The proof of the pudding is in the eating; the tree is known by its fruit. Even if we can accurately identify the moment in which we passed from death to life, there are other necessary indications of true salvation.

After considering all these inconclusive indications, you may feel shaken, troubled, exposed—even devastated. Please remember that while I have no desire to trouble true saints, there is almost nothing more dangerous than to imagine oneself saved and yet remain unsaved. Neither is it healthy for true children of God to establish their confidence on beams that will give way in time of trouble and testing. We need to know the truth, and we do well to know it by right means. If you seek to reach heaven except by the way of the cross, you are mistaken, and you must be put right. It is better for unbelievers to know they are under the curse now than on the day of judgment. Better to discover now that we are confused as to the basis of our assurance than in the day of trial.

By the same token, there is nothing more blessed than to know we are Christians grounded on a solid foundation, as the Spirit witnesses in our hearts and to the work He is accomplishing in those whom He indwells. To recognize these inconclusive indications for what they are liberates the true believer from the tyranny of mere subjectivism and strips away the flawed and rotten supports on which we—and others—too often build our hopes.

Indispensable Indications

What, then, are the scriptural indicators that a genuine work of grace has taken place in the sinner's heart? If we find that these inconclusive indications may and often should be in the saints but might be also in the unconverted, what are the marks that invariably demonstrate the presence of everlasting life? To obtain the right answers, we must ask the right questions.

When the apostle John writes his letter, he does so in carefully planned circles. Like an aircraft circling the same territory, John notes the same heart terrain repeatedly. As John covers his ground, several conclusive marks of genuine spiritual life become evident. These can be the result only of the Holy Spirit's saving operations on a sinful heart; they simply do not exist in an unconverted person. If you have them in development, you are in Christ; if you lack them in total, you are not. They are the fruits of Christ's saving work for us and the Spirit's saving work in us and are never found apart from the redeeming acts of the triune God. At least four indispensable indications of true Christianity become plain as we circle through John's letter.

Repentance and Faith

The first indication is a humble and wholehearted embrace of the divine diagnosis of and remedy for sin.[3] A Christian man has an accurate view of himself as a sinning sinner. He acknowledges the just judgments of a holy God (Ps. 51:4; Luke 15:18; 18:13). Sin is no longer abstract and general but concrete and specific. Like the prodigal son, he comes to himself and confesses his sin (Luke 15:17–18); like the tax collector in the temple, he is humbled before God and owns his true character and need. Remember that we have already said that conviction alone is not conclusive, but neither is it to be lightly dismissed. The issue is not the degree but the effect of conviction. Many read of Christians who underwent

---

3. You can see John's cumulative evidence for this in 1 John 1:7–2:2; 2:12–14; 3:5–6, 23; 4:2, 9–10, 13–16; 5:1, 5, 10–13, 20.

prolonged and agonizing experience of conviction before obtaining peace and wonder if this is required. Some who have grown up under the restraint of true gospel influence do not always feel the same terrors as those arrested in some profane course of life. Others find that their sense of sin after conversion is far more intense than it was before they were saved, and so they wonder if they are really saved. We must distinguish between what is descriptive and prescriptive. There are few who enter the kingdom without a degree of often vigorous conviction; there are none who become citizens without coming to know it more or less. In some it is gradual and deliberate, in others sudden and intense (compare Lydia and the Philippian jailer—Acts 16:11–15 and 25–34). Some ask, "How much conviction is enough?" The Bible gives us no percentage! Enough to bring you to the end of yourself and to Christ.

This is because Spirit-wrought conviction of sin leads to genuine repentance as a sinner's heart breaks over his godlessness. This is where Saul, Ahab, Judas, and Felix fell short. They were full of guilt, regret, remorse, and fear. They knew that God was angered and that they deserved punishment, but we do not read that—despite mourning and trembling—they truly repented. Repentance is more than regret, and it is certainly not despair. Repentance recognizes not just the effects of sin on us (rendering us liable to judgment) but also takes full account of sin in itself, in all its foulness and filthiness. Repentance sees sin as it is in the eyes of God and in relation to His holiness. It involves revulsion over sin, heartbrokenness over iniquity, and a sense of its offensiveness to God as obnoxious to His holiness.

When we see this we may feel that we need to repent of our repentance, but we must also notice the direction in which repentance travels. It flees not from God but to God, seeing in Him a readiness to forgive. In Psalm 51:4 David is dealing with God; the prodigal in Luke 15:18 is planning to speak to his father; the tax collector is before God in His temple (Luke 18:10). The Lord said through Joel:

"Now, therefore," says the LORD,
"Turn to Me with all your heart,
With fasting, with weeping, and with mourning."
So rend your heart, and not your garments;
Return to the LORD *your God,*
For He is gracious and merciful,
Slow to anger, and of great kindness;
And He relents from doing harm. (Joel 2:12–13)

True repentance involves a conviction of sin that is God-drenched rather than man-centered, which makes a person turn his back on sin and draws his heart out to God, desiring to be freed from sin and found in the way of obedience.

It is this that sends the repenting person to his Savior. Faith is the twin grace of repentance. They are sisters who walk everywhere hand in hand. Repentance lets go of sin just as faith lays hold on Christ. Faith is not exercised in a vacuum. "Do you have faith?" is a nonsense question, for faith needs an object. Neither is faith mere belief in certain data (cf. James 2:19). Saving faith has as its object the Lord Jesus Christ as He is presented to us in the gospel; it knows, receives, takes, and relies upon Him as He is so presented.

So much confusion enters when people become more concerned with assurance than with Christ. The problem is that assurance does not save. Not even faith saves in itself. It is Christ who saves by faith. Faith is not the belief that we are saved but the belief that we are lost which sends us fleeing to Christ to save us. The question is not if we are elect but rather if we are trusting in Christ, for faith is the sure evidence of our election rather than election the warrant for our faith (John 6:29; 1 John 5:1). In the words of William Gurnall,

> It is plain, we are not to make election a ground for our faith, but our faith and calling a medium or argument to prove our election. Election indeed is first in order of divine acting. God chooses before we believe, yet faith is first in our acting. We must believe before we can know we are elected; indeed,

by believing we know it.... You may know you are elect, as
surely by a work of grace in you, as if you had stood by God's
elbow when he wrote your name in the book of life.[4]

It is a terrible and tragic thing to see someone trapped and tor-
mented by the felt uncertainty of his or her election. Sometimes
unconverted men or women are entangled by the fear that they
are not elect, and so they are kept from simply believing in Christ,
working on the notion that until they know they are elect, it would
be unrighteous to believe on the premise that only the elect have
faith. Sometimes it might be a true believer who is being assaulted
on this matter, weak of faith and doubting his election, and therefore finding faith further undermined on the premise that if God
has not chosen me, then I cannot have believed. But the doctrine
of election was never intended to hinder the repentant or cripple
the weak. To be sure, God's sovereign grace is magnified by the
doctrine of election, and election can and should be preached as
such, but the gospel call is not the call to know that you are elect
but the command to repent and believe in Christ, for whoever
truly does that is, by definition, one of God's chosen ones. As
such, election becomes not the enemy of assurance but one of its
greatest supporters, underpinning our confidence in God and our
pursuit of godliness.

So saving faith has Christ in view: it comprehends Jesus of
Nazareth as God's Lord and Christ and yields itself to Him as the
only and sufficient Savior of sinners. It commits itself entirely to
His covenant care and keeping as the God-man, the one Mediator
between God and men, the Redeemer, the blood-soaked Substitute,
the atoning Lamb who takes away sin. Faith considers Christ in all
His might and majesty, in all His meekness and mercy, and casts
itself upon Him for time and eternity. Remember John Owen's
masterful description: faith receives Jesus, looks to Jesus, comes to
Jesus, flees to Jesus, leans upon Jesus, trusts in Jesus, holds to Jesus,

---

4. William Gurnall, *The Christian in Complete Armour* (Edinburgh: Banner of
Truth, 1964), 96. The language has been slightly updated.

and rests upon Jesus. In short, it is the renunciation of all hope and help in self and other creatures and a going out of the soul to Christ for the life in Him, comprehending and apprehending in Him all the blessings of salvation (Eph. 1:9–23). Faith brings us into and keeps us in union with Jesus so that all God has put in and with Him becomes ours. This is why we must come to full-orbed views of what we are and have in Christ—because life is found in Him, and all its fixed blessings and fruitful evidences flow out of our relationship with Him.

The question, then, is this: Are you now repenting and trusting in Jesus as a needy sinner? Not, "Did you once do this?" as a sudden regret or temporary concern, but, "Are you now?" as a present reality? If so, life is yours in Christ Jesus. Remember that this is the essential point and gives birth to all that follows. The dying thief never had an opportunity to manifest the other marks of saving faith (though he would have done so had he lived), but still the Lord assured him, "Today you will be with Me in Paradise" (Luke 23:43). He was as much a saved man as the apostle John was when he wrote his gospel and letters, because both men were trusting in the same Jesus. Whoever trusts in Jesus, though he believes one moment and dies the next, has his life hid with Christ in God. It is not the strength of your faith that saves, but the Christ to whom faith looks. If we have no opportunity to do anything before death but believe, we are safe.

In summary, every true child of God demonstrates a humble and wholehearted embrace of the divine diagnosis of and remedy for sin. He has come to an accurately low view of himself as a sinning sinner and to an accurately high view of Christ Jesus as a sufficient Savior and—under the irresistible influence of the Holy Spirit—has acted rightly in accordance with these convictions.

Devotion to God

Another indispensable indication is a humble reverence for and joyful devotion to God and His glory.[5] As I have already said, when someone becomes a Christian, everything changes (2 Cor. 5:17). In union with Christ, we have died to sin and risen again to walk in newness of life (Rom. 6:4–13). As a result, a radical reversal of perspective and priority has occurred: the idol self is toppled from the throne of our hearts, and every subsidiary and supplementary idol has been renounced absolutely in principle and increasingly in practice. Tim Challies says,

> Sin is inherently anti-God, inherently pro-self. Each time I sin I make a statement about myself and a statement about (and against) God. Each time I sin, I declare my own independence, my own desire to be rid of God; I declare that I can do better than God, that I can be a better god than God…. When I am god, I am enslaved. When God is God, I am free. I thank God that God is God.[6]

The true believer, one possessing eternal life, thanks God that God is God. The Lord reigns supreme on the soul-throne. The heart that by nature is enmity with God (Rom. 8:7) has been replaced by one that loves God entirely (Luke 10:27), issuing in humble reverence and joyful devotion. He no longer defines God in relation to himself but himself in relation to God. This, too, must be of the Holy Ghost.

The person with a new heart has *a new and true perception of God*. He considers God as almighty Creator, in whom we all live and move and have our being (Acts 17:25, 28), who made and sustains all things (John 1:1–3; 2 Peter 3:5). With the prophets and psalmists he sees the work of God's hands in all things, declaring, "In the beginning, God…." He considers God as an all-gracious

---

5. Consider the cumulative evidence of 1 John 1:3–5; 2:12–15; 3:1–2; 4:12–13, 19; 5:1–2.

6. Tim Challies, "When I Am God," *Challies.com* (blog), March 19, 2012, http://www.challies.com/christian-living/when-i-am-god.

Redeemer who has acted of His own free purpose to save a people for Himself and who sent His Son to suffer and die for sinners so that those who believe might say, He "loved me and gave Himself for me" (Gal. 2:20). In this, God is proved just and the justifier of the one who believes in Jesus (Rom. 3:26), all this being done to the praise of His glorious grace (Eph. 1:6). The Christian concurs with John Murray that "God appeases His own holy wrath in the cross of Christ in order that the purpose of his love to lost men may be accomplished in accordance with and to the vindication of all the perfections that constitute his glory"[7] and would have it no other way. He considers God an all-glorious Lord, who sits in the heavens and does what He pleases (Pss. 115:3; 135:5–6) and is glad it should be so, that God in Christ may have the preeminence (Col. 1:18). He reads Romans 11:36—"For of Him and through Him and to Him are all things, to whom be glory forever"—and asks, "How could anything else be proper?" adding his own resounding "Amen!" The utter loveliness of the God who has loved the unlovely compels sincere adoration (1 John 4:19–5:2).

Furthermore, this person has *a new and true perspective on self.* With God enthroned, the child of God sees himself as a dependent creature in a posture of absolute reliance. Like Job confronted with the majesty of God in the whirlwind, he repents of his proud self-determination in dust and ashes. He sees the heavens declare the glory of the Lord (Ps. 19:1), considers the works of His fingers and is humbled (Ps. 8:3), and is conscious that the very being of men hangs upon the Lord (Acts 17:25, 28; Rom. 9:20). He knows that all strength comes from Him, that every good gift is His to bestow (James 1:17). Furthermore, the child of God perceives himself as a needy sinner in a relationship of entire dependence and obligation. Dead in trespasses and sins by nature, he has been raised from the dead to sit in the heavenlies with Christ; a child of wrath, he has been adopted into the family of God. Like Mephibosheth before

---

7. John Murray, *Redemption Accomplished and Applied* (Edinburgh: Banner of Truth, 2009), 25.

David, he wonders, "What is your servant, that you should look upon such a dead dog as I?" (2 Sam. 9:8). He recognizes that by grace he has been saved, and every blessing must be traced up the stream to the fountain—that all spiritual life comes from the Lord. He further owns himself to be an adopted son and a willing servant bound to total obedience. Like Isaiah in the temple, he offers himself: "Here am I! Send me" (Isa. 6:8). Like Saul on the Damascus road, overcome by the glory of God shining in the face of Jesus Christ, he can only ask, "Lord, what do You want me to do?" (Acts 9:6), recognizing that the life he now lives he must live by faith in the Son of God, who loved him and gave Himself for him (Gal. 2:20). All the life and strength that comes from Him is for Him, and if it all were expended in the cause of Christ he remains an unprofitable servant who has done simply what was his duty to do (Luke 17:10). He can sing without a shadow of doubt,

> *What is my being but for Thee,*
> *Its sure support, its noblest end?*[8]

He desires, like the incarnate Son, that God may be all in all (1 Cor. 15:28).

And all this issues in *a new and true devotion to God*. It is in the space between our perceptions of God and of ourselves that true religion develops. In John Calvin's words, "True and solid Wisdom consists almost entirely of two parts: the knowledge of God and of ourselves,"[9] for between these two points we see increasingly His utter worthiness and our grounds for devotion. These things increase over time. Trace the trajectory of Paul's sense of these things. In 1 Corinthians 15:9–10 he is "the least of the apostles, who am not worthy to be called an apostle, because I persecuted the church of God. But by the grace of God I am what I am, and His grace toward me was not in vain." By the point at which he writes Ephesians 3:8 he is saying, "To me, who am less than the

---

8. Philip Doddridge, "My Gracious Lord, I Own Thy Right."
9. John Calvin, *The Institutes of the Christian Religion,* ed. John T. McNeill, trans. Ford Lewis Battles (Philadelphia: Westminster, 1960), 1.1.1.

least of all the saints, this grace was given, that I should preach among the Gentiles the unsearchable riches of Christ." Toward the end of his life, in 1 Timothy 1:15–16, he is proclaiming "a faithful saying and worthy of all acceptance, that Christ Jesus came into the world to save sinners, of whom I am chief. However, for this reason I obtained mercy, that in me first Jesus Christ might show all long-suffering, as a pattern to those who are going to believe on Him for everlasting life." Do you see how Paul's sense of God's majesty, Christ's sufficiency, and his own need all advanced as he made his way through life, keeping pace with each other? The greater God appears, the lower self appears, and the gap is filled with gratitude, humility, earnestness, love, and zeal.

So the one who possesses eternal life once lived for self but now lives for God. His gratitude for the grace he has received mingles with and enhances his conviction of and delight in God's manifest excellence for its own sake and calls for a life of living sacrifice (Rom. 12:1–2). If there were no reward, no heaven, he would still delight in God, because God is delightful in Himself. He seeks to live a life with God at the core and peak in his thinking and feeling and doing.

Surely such a disposition is part of the testimony of the Spirit of adoption, witnessing with our spirits that we are the children of God. When a soul begins to breathe out such desires, from whom else could they proceed? It is one of those spiritual curiosities that the times when we most feel our unworthiness and unfitness for God are often those times when He is drawing closest to us. It is often when we are most humbled on account of our sin and feel our wretchedness that we enjoy the sweet breath of the Spirit upon our hearts, enabling us to cry out, "Abba, Father" (Rom. 8:15).

The testimony of such a man's heart is,

> *Whom have I in heaven but you?*
> *And there is none upon earth that I desire besides You.*
> *My flesh and my heart fail;*
> *But God is the strength of my heart and my portion forever.*
> (Ps. 73:25–26)

It takes little prompting to reveal that he is one who proclaims the praises of Him who called him out of darkness into His marvelous light (1 Peter 2:9). He prays,

> *Our Father in heaven,*
> *Hallowed be Your name.*
> *Your kingdom come.*
> *Your will be done*
> *On earth as it is in heaven....*
> *For Yours is the kingdom and the power and the glory forever.*
> (Matt. 6:9–13)

And then, for he is no hypocrite, he willingly consecrates his time, energies, gifts, graces, faculties, and efforts to this great end, however insignificant or otherwise such labors may appear (1 Cor. 10:31). When he is asked, "What is the chief end of man?" he replies, in words or in sense, "Man's chief end is to glorify God and to enjoy Him forever," weeping tears of shame and joy that such sentiments as these might be sincerely formed on the lips of such a wretch as himself. God in Christ is all in all to him, and he longs to know and feel and prove it more.

Growth in Holiness

The third indication is a principled pursuit of godliness with an increasing attainment in that holiness[10] "without which no one will see the Lord" (Heb. 12:14), for how "can two walk together, unless they are agreed?" (Amos 3:3). The hypocrite is content with the mere name of holiness, but the Christian seeks its true nature. A child of the world may be pleased with a reputation for holiness, but the true child of God is satisfied only with the reality. A Christian does not seek to cover his sin but to be cured of it. The one who makes the grace of God an excuse to go on sinning is using the devil's reasoning and is no true saint (Rom. 6:1). When a person is converted, self is dethroned, God is enthroned, the world loses its domination, the chains of sin are broken, and—repenting

---

10. Feel the weight of 1 John 2:3–8, 15–16, 19, 29; 3:3, 6, 10, 24; 4:13; 5:2–5, 21.

of his sins daily, even hourly—the believer seeks to walk by faith in newness of life, and that newness of life works out in obedience to God.

Behind this lies a driving principle: "Everyone who has this hope in Him purifies himself, just as He is pure" (1 John 3:3). A Christian's former fundamental attachment to sin and persistent habit of shameless, unrepentant sinning has been shattered as a result of his union with the living Christ (Rom. 6:8–14). The new root produces new fruit: "A good tree cannot bear bad fruit, nor can a bad tree bear good fruit. Every tree that does not bear good fruit is cut down and thrown into the fire. Therefore by their fruits you will know them" (Matt. 7:18–20; cf. 12:32–35). That is why John identifies the one who goes on in the habit of sinning as no true saint (notice that he is not talking about an absolute and entire absence of sin, but rather an end to the pattern of continuing carelessly in sin).

Love for the world is dead under the shadow of the cross (Gal. 6:14; James 4:4); conformity to the world, company with it, and compromise for it are no longer the Christian's appetite (1 Cor. 15:33; 2 Tim. 3:4). Paul impresses upon the church at Corinth the fact that holiness is not an optional extra in Christian living but an indispensable element of it:

Do not be unequally yoked together with unbelievers. For what fellowship has righteousness with lawlessness? And what communion has light with darkness? And what accord has Christ with Belial? Or what part has a believer with an unbeliever? And what agreement has the temple of God with idols? For you are the temple of the living God. As God has said:

"I will dwell in them
And walk among them.
I will be their God,
And they shall be My people."
Therefore "Come out from among them
And be separate, says the Lord.
Do not touch what is unclean,

And I will receive you."
"I will be a Father to you,
And you shall be My sons and daughters,
Says the LORD Almighty." (2 Cor. 6:14–18)

In 1 Corinthians 5 and 6, Paul writes that these saints had been enmeshed before conversion in some public, heinous sins (1 Cor. 6:9–10) and were struggling to break free from those patterns. In 2 Corinthians 6, he uses the language of the temple, God's dwelling place on earth, to emphasize the divine demand for holiness, using a chain of Old Testament quotations to make his point (Leviticus 26:12 with Exodus 29:45, pressed home with Isaiah 52:11, Ezekiel 20:34, and Isaiah 43:6 with 2 Samuel 7:14).

All of this builds to that affectionate but potent entreaty of 2 Corinthians 7:1: "Therefore, having these promises, beloved, let us cleanse ourselves from all filthiness of the flesh and spirit, perfecting holiness in the fear of God." The redeemed person is one who, because God in Christ by the Spirit indwells him, makes a complete break with sin and all compromise with an unhealthy attachment to the world in order to pursue holiness in the fear of the Lord. This is John's point—this is a mark of everlasting life. Until we are joined to Christ, we cannot and will not do it; once we are alive in Christ, it follows as an inevitable consequence.

This is not walling yourself off from the world (1 Cor. 5:10; cf. Matt. 5:14–16). It is a call to holiness both negatively and positively. Negatively, it involves stripping off, putting to death, and leaving behind all iniquity of body and soul. It is the deliberate and determined avoidance, rejection, and destruction of all that belongs to the realm of darkness, within and without. But it is more than the absence of sin, for—positively—it involves pursuing, embracing, and cultivating all righteousness of body and soul.[11] It is the deliberate and determined desire for and cultivation

---

11. See Romans 6:13; 13:12; Galatians 5:19–25; Ephesians 4:22–24; 5:11; Colossians 3:8–14; 1 Peter 2:1–2. Please take the opportunity at some point to trace out these negative and positive aspects of godliness side by side.

of all that belongs to the kingdom of God, within and without, in thought, word, and deed.[12]

As redeemed sinners we are called out of the world and to God in every aspect and facet of life, putting off and putting on, putting away and bringing in, slaying sin and stirring up life. In doing this we have a divine pattern. This is astounding—even overwhelming: "Everyone who has this hope in Him purifies himself, just as He is pure" (1 John 3:3). Peter confirms the same: "Therefore gird up the loins of your mind, be sober, and rest your hope fully upon the grace that is to be brought to you at the revelation of Jesus Christ; as obedient children, not conforming yourselves to the former lusts, as in your ignorance; but as He who called you is holy, you also be holy in all your conduct, because it is written, 'Be holy, for I am holy'" (1 Peter 1:13–16). This is what sets the believer apart from the merely moral or outwardly religious. We do not define goodness for ourselves in accordance with our own notions, but we follow a pattern; one who has no desire for, delight in, and determination toward godliness as defined and demonstrated by God Himself is simply not a Christian.

What does this look like on the human level? It looks like Jesus Christ. It is to Him that we are being conformed (Rom. 8:29). He is God incarnate, godliness embodied (John 4:34; 6:38). The ready obedience of consistent, conscious, comprehensive godliness is patterned in Christ and obtained only in union with Him. This was the Lord's own prayer for His people: "I do not pray that You should take them out of the world, but that You should keep them from the evil one. They are not of the world, just as I am not of the world. Sanctify them by Your truth. Your word is truth. As You sent Me into the world, I also have sent them into the world. And for their sakes I sanctify Myself, that they also may be sanctified by the truth" (John 17:15–19).

---

12. See Titus 2:12–14; cf. 1 John 2:6–7, 15–17, 29; 3:3–4, 6, 10, 24; 5:3–5, 21. Again, please read these texts to see the comparisons and contrasts contained within them.

With such a pattern before us, the work of holiness becomes *a deliberate pursuit.* No part of life escapes this demand. This is not a pursuit only for Sundays, around Christians and before other people, but it consumes us at all times and in all circumstances before God. Godliness should mark us without exception of time, place, and company. It is not like when someone comes to our filthy house and we sweep all the muck under the carpets and push all the rubbish into the cupboards. It is a life in which every room is open to inspection as a place where the pursuit of purity is in full swing.

The child of God follows Peter's command: "You also be holy in all your conduct" (1 Peter 1:15). The Christian takes up his cross daily and follows his Master on the path to the end (Matt. 16:24–25). D. A. Carson reminds us that

> people do not drift toward holiness. Apart from grace-driven effort, people do not gravitate toward godliness, prayer, obedience to Scripture, faith and delight in Christ. We drift toward compromise and call it tolerance; we drift toward disobedience and call it freedom; we drift toward superstition and call it faith. We cherish the indiscipline of lost self-control and call it relaxation; we slouch toward prayerlessness and delude ourselves into thinking we have escaped legalism; we slide toward godlessness and convince ourselves that we have been liberated.[13]

Here the life in the saint is manifest: he knows that if he drifts it will be toward sin, so he drives toward godliness. Paul exhorts us, as we shall see in a later chapter, to make sure that the realities of salvation are pressed into all our existence, kneading the yeast of godliness into the dough of life. The sincere believer considers his ways and turns his feet back to God's testimonies (Ps. 119:59). He is concerned that such obedience is extended through the whole of his redeemed humanity, regular and consistent, willing rather than forced, and maintained to the end.

---

13. D. A. Carson, *For the Love of God, Volume 2* (Wheaton, Ill.: Crossway, 2006), January 23 reading.

At this point you might be tempted to throw up your hands and say, "If that is the standard, then it is all over for me!" Perhaps this sounds like the counsel of despair. If so, we must consider carefully that what we are looking to see is a discernible progress.

The mark of a saint is *not* present, sinless perfection. John himself says that anyone who claims to be without sin, past or present, is self-deceived (1 John 1:8, 10). The mark that we seek is the principled pursuit of godliness with increasing attainment in holiness: arduous, laborious, but genuine progress over time. It is never promised to be easy or painless. On the contrary, it is both hard and painful. Christ does not promise no battles but rather great battles against fierce enemies, opposed as He now is to a raging and committed foe of malice and power (Rom. 7:13–25; Eph. 6:10), but the battle itself is the very evidence of life. Consider two examples of this in poetry. The first comes from John Newton and is a painfully honest account of sanctification by a man who had once fondly hoped it would happen easily:

> *I asked the Lord that I might grow*
> *In faith, and love, and every grace;*
> *Might more of his salvation know,*
> *And seek, more earnestly, his face.*
>
> *'Twas he who taught me thus to pray,*
> *And he, I trust, has answered prayer!*
> *But it has been in such a way,*
> *As almost drove me to despair.*
>
> *I hoped that in some favoured hour,*
> *At once he'd answer my request;*
> *And by his love's constraining pow'r,*
> *Subdue my sins, and give me rest.*
>
> *Instead of this, he made me feel*
> *The hidden evils of my heart;*
> *And let the angry pow'rs of hell*
> *Assault my soul in every part.*

> *Yea more, with his own hand he seemed*
> *Intent to aggravate my woe;*
> *Crossed all the fair designs I schemed,*
> *Blasted my gourds, and laid me low.*
>
> *Lord, why is this, I trembling cried,*
> *Wilt thou pursue thy worm to death?*
> *"'Tis in this way," the Lord replied,*
> *"I answer prayer for grace and faith."*
>
> *"These inward trials I employ,*
> *From self, and pride, to set thee free;*
> *And break thy schemes of earthly joy,*
> *That thou may'st find thy all in me."*

Newton's conclusion is not how we might wish it to be, but it is true. Another man, Joseph Hart, puts it more briefly in a poem called *The Paradox*:

> *How strange is the course that a Christian must steer!*
> *How perplext is the path he must tread!*
> *The hope of his happiness rises from fear,*
> *And his life he receives from the dead.*
>
> *His fairest pretensions must wholly be wav'd,*
> *And his best resolutions be crost;*
> *Nor can he expect to be perfectly sav'd,*
> *Till he finds himself utterly lost.*
>
> *When all this is done, and his heart is assur'd*
> *Of the total remission of sins;*
> *When his pardon is sign'd, and his peace is procur'd,*
> *From that moment his conflict begins.*

The only reason that a person fights is that he is in Christ. The willing and the doing find their root in God's work in the heart (Phil. 2:12–13; cf. Col: 2:6).

So if you plot the points of the Christian's life on a graph, it is not a smooth, uniform, upward slope, any more than the Allied triumph over Hitler's Nazis can be traced by steady and unwavering movements across a map. Rather, there are painful reverses, agonizing declines, turgid plateaus. However, over time, the line of best fit shows an upward, onward trajectory. Sometimes, yes, the Christian wanders; sometimes he is on the defensive; sometimes, grievously, he backslides. But the tone and tenor of his life is advance, the pattern is of sins repented over and slaughtered (1 John 1:9–2:2), of godliness cultivated. It is seen in the weakening of his sinful lusts and desires, in the vigor of the battle, in sinning less often, repenting more readily, returning less frequently to sins, manifesting the fruit of the Spirit. In all these marks of true salvation, we must ask not just, "Where am I now?" but also, "How far have I come?"

And remember that none of this takes place apart from the reality of the new birth and the indwelling of the Holy Spirit. If this is your experience in measure, it can only be because the Spirit of Christ is at work in you. It would never happen naturally; it must be a fruit of the life of God in the soul of man. If you can see these marks of a new life in you, springing up in the bud, even if not yet in full bloom, do not deny their origin but rejoice in what they are: the signs of the life of the Spirit and a sure indicator of what is to come: "For whom He foreknew, He also predestined to be conformed to the image of His Son, that He might be the firstborn among many brethren. Moreover whom He predestined, these He also called; whom He called, these He also justified; and whom He justified, these He also glorified" (Rom. 8:29–30).

Love for the Saints

As we have seen and will see in more detail, the saints are works in progress. God loved all true believers even while they were altogether unlovely—this is the marvel of His grace (Ezek. 16:1–14; Rom. 5:8–10; Eph. 2:4–7). That divine love is working on us to make us lovely, so that one day—when faith is sight—every saint will be entirely conformed to the image of God in Christ, being like Him when we see Him as He is (1 John 3:1–2), to the praise of

His glory. And in this time between the ages, in this "already" / "not yet" tension, another indispensable indication of true Christianity is demonstrated: affection for and attachment to God's redeemed people.[14] Every true saint in whom there is everlasting life is one who loves other saints. We are not called to love the presently perfect but the imperfect—the other works in progress.

There are many empty professions of love. This love is not a matter of mere presence or nearness—an accidental or coincidental proximity. Just because you happen to be among God's people does not mean that you are one of them, any more than a goat among the sheep ceases to be a goat and simply becomes a sheep or gets treated as one. Goats must be made sheep in order to inherit eternal life. Simply getting to the right places at the right times in order to mingle with sheep is not love.

Neither is love mere natural affection. Because saints are works in progress, progress has been made. All of us require much more clearing of weeds and growing of fruit, but often the development of Christlikeness makes Christians, in many respects, pleasing company. The rough edges are being smoothed down, and there is an ease, warmth, and humility, a kindness and acceptance, that make the saints likeable on many levels. A morose, bitter, and sullen Christian ought to be a contradiction in terms (do we not wish it were altogether so!), but a healthy saint—apart from what some will consider those annoying tendencies to talk about the Lord Jesus, to refuse to bend the rules to suit the circumstances, and to insist that people need to be saved—might be a pleasant companion. There may be other attachments, ties of family and friendship, which enhance this sense. But liking the saints is not necessarily a sign of life.

Neither is love a mercenary attachment. Again, growing believers are humble and generous, following Christ in doing good to all, especially to the household of faith. Under such circumstances a

---

14. Consider the following passages in 1 John on this matter: 2:9–11; 3:10–18, 23; 4:7–11; 4:20–5:2.

Christian might be regarded as a soft touch. I know a man who comes up to open-air preachers in the town in which I live, spends a minute telling them about how much he loves Jesus, and then produces a shopping list. Although they might not be quite so brazen, some people attach themselves to the church because of what they think they can get out of it, whether in terms of respect, kindness, material benefits, or because it seems relatively easy to become a big shot when everyone else is seeking to be a servant. But this is not an indication of new life.

Neither is love a party spirit, a sort of gang mentality. Some want to belong to what is considered the right denomination, community, or coalition—or, at least, the biggest, richest, most powerful, or fastest growing. Some like to be part of a crowd. How often among a group of young people are there those who, when some are converted, make a profession of faith so as not to be left out? Some like a sense of belonging, of camaraderie, a bit like supporting a certain sports team: we all wear the same uniform, sing the same songs, go to the same gatherings, and so enjoy a measure of security. Some know what the church is against (or think they do, maybe having no idea what the church is genuinely for) and join up because they are against the same. Some just like a good fight or debate, and the church can seem a good place to find one or start one; others are looking for a little intellectual stimulation or people with the right kind of behavior. But this is hardly love for the saints as God defines it.

But if none of these are what we seek, what are the genuine reasons for love of the brothers? The godly love that marks a true child of God is fashioned by our experience of being loved:

> Beloved, let us love one another, for love is of God; and everyone who loves is born of God and knows God. He who does not love does not know God, for God is love. In this the love of God was manifested toward us, that God has sent His only begotten Son into the world, that we might live through Him. In this is love, not that we loved God, but that He loved us and sent His Son to be the propitiation for our

sins. Beloved, if God so loved us, we also ought to love one another. (1 John 4:7–11)

We learn to love by being loved; that love then becomes the pattern for our loving. I have heard preacher and theologian Sinclair Ferguson say that we will be to others what we believe God has been to us. If this is so, how many of us would do well to spend more time meditating upon God's love to us in Christ? If we cannot imagine or accept being loved while unlovely, if we do not believe that we have been so loved, we will find it hard to replicate this love toward others (and so lack of assurance might become a vicious circle). Only the person who has been loved with God's love can begin to love with something approximating God's love.

Modeling this love, the true child of God loves other believers because of what they are to God: *beloved*. He has loved them with an everlasting love, with an unshakeable and all-conquering love, showering them with His grace in Christ Jesus. They are His begotten sons (1 John 5:1), the redeemed objects of Christ's atoning work. It is like God to love those whom God loves—it is godliness. You may have some obnoxious nieces or nephews, some difficult cousins, some quarrelsome grandchildren, or whatever else, but you have an affection for them as a reflection of your affection for your brothers and sisters, your own children, your friends. So with us: we see the saints as beloved by God, and so we love them ourselves. God declares His people to be the excellent of the earth despite their remaining sin, and the renewed soul concurs in that judgment, however much it may struggle with the outworking of it.

The true child of God also loves other believers because of what they are in themselves. The image of God is being stamped into them, the likeness of Christ is increasingly evident in them, and the Holy Spirit's indwelling is growing plain in them. They are becoming holy as God is holy, purifying themselves just as He is pure, and that draws out the heart of the one who is himself learning to love God and godliness. He discerns in his brothers and sisters something of God. So, as those children we mentioned above mature, we hope to see in their physique, character, and habits the likeness of the One whom we love, and it draws out our heart further. They are a chip off the old block, and because you love the old block, you love the chip. True religion delights you, and it delights you as you see it increasingly in the lives of other saints.

But you also love true believers because of what they are to you: fellow members of the body of which Christ Jesus Himself is the head (1 Cor. 12:12–14, 26–27); fellow soldiers of the cross fighting under the same banner; fellow pilgrims on the heavenly way; fellow wrestlers with sin; encouragers, helpers, exhorters, mutual assistants along the road, and shared inheritors in the glory to come (Col. 1:12). They are heirs of God, coheirs with Christ, joint heirs with you.

This love, grounded in such realities, is the love of a true child of God, and there are always sincere expressions of love: "My little children, let us not love in word or in tongue, but in deed and in truth" (1 John 3:18). Love is always demonstrated, finding its pattern in the love of Christ with which we have been loved. It has real objects: other people with remaining sin, deep needs, awkward qualities—people just like you. You see it in its essence and scope in 1 Corinthians 13: "Love suffers long and is kind; love does not envy; love does not parade itself, is not puffed up; does not behave rudely, does not seek its own, is not provoked, thinks no evil; does not rejoice in iniquity, but rejoices in the truth; bears all things, believes all things, hopes all things, endures all things. Love never fails" (vv. 4–8).

Paul traces some of the contours of this love in Ephesians 4: "Walk worthy of the calling with which you were called, with all lowliness and gentleness, with longsuffering, bearing with one another in love, endeavoring to keep the unity of the Spirit in the bond of peace. There is one body and one Spirit, just as you were called in one hope of your calling; one Lord, one faith, one baptism; one God and Father of all, who is above all, and through all, and in you all" (vv. 1–6).

In the verses that follow, he takes up some of what this means. He speaks of the ministers the risen Christ has given to His church for the equipping and edifying of the saints, pressing on toward "the unity of the faith and of the knowledge of the Son of God." These men labor for the spiritual and doctrinal maturity of God's people, so that as they speak "the truth in love," believers "may grow up in all things into Him who is the head—Christ—from whom the whole body, joined and knit together by what every joint supplies, according to the effective working by which every part does its share, causes growth of the body for the edifying of itself in love" (vv. 11–16). Love lies at the very heart of the corporate life of the church of Jesus Christ. As Paul proceeds, he emphasizes that this love has an abidingly practical face: it has no place for lying to one another, for expressions of sinful anger, for laziness and theft, for corrupt and cutting speech that imparts no grace to those who hear it. He focuses on the Holy Spirit and excludes from a faithful and fruitful Christian walk all those manifestations of a sinful heart, expressed primarily through speech, that are contrary to the Spirit's work in the believer as He operates to form Christ in them: "Let all bitterness, wrath, anger, clamor, and evil speaking be put away from you, with all malice. And be kind to one another, tenderhearted, forgiving one another, just as God in Christ forgave you" (vv. 25–32). Again, such love is patterned in God Himself and has about it the savor of Christ Jesus:

> Therefore if there is any consolation in Christ, if any comfort of love, if any fellowship of the Spirit, if any affection and mercy, fulfill my joy by being like-minded, having the same love, being of one accord, of one mind. Let nothing be done through selfish ambition or conceit, but in lowliness of mind let each esteem others better than himself. Let each of you look out not only for his own interests, but also for the interests of others.
>
> Let this mind be in you which was also in Christ Jesus. (Phil. 2:1–5)

This is a spiritual, universal, appropriate, and constant love manifested in our attitudes and actions, our convictions and commitments, in our forbearing and forgiving, in our speech and our service, in our affection and investment.

And I hope it will not be too obvious if I suggest that it is, by definition, a corporate grace. Christian love cannot fly solo but needs real objects—it needs the church. Christians who think that they can get by without the church are suspect, because they may be saying that they do not need or cannot be sure of the love of other saints or that they cannot find anyone whom they are willing to love. (Note that being genuinely unable to find a faithful church is different from not bothering to look for a church.) The arena for Christian love is the church, and the healthy saint delights to be there. He is a true churchman: he does not simply "do church"—he is part of the church. He is concerned for the immediate and distant children of God, taken up with the church's local and global well-being. He is no mere spectator but is a wholeheartedly engaged servant. He does not ask first, "What can I get out of this?" but "What can I put into it?" And in the exercise of love and its accompanying graces, he finds his heart made sure, as he supports, serves, prays for and with, protects, preserves, attends, and delights in the church of his Lord Jesus.

If you have no regard for God's people, you are not part of God's people. But are you perhaps fearful? Do you feel presumptuous to seek baptism and membership? And yet the testimony of your heart is this: "As for the saints who are on the earth, 'they are the excellent ones, in whom is all my delight'" (Ps. 16:3). The desire of your heart is expressed in this way:

> For a day in Your courts is better than a thousand.
> I would rather be a doorkeeper in the house of my God
> Than dwell in the tents of wickedness. (Ps. 84:10)

You love the character and company of God's people: their thoughts, aims, desires, and hopes chime with yours. Why? Is it not that you belong among them? God's children love and long to take their place in His family. Here, and only here, are they truly at home in this fallen world.

Holding Up the Mirror

These four marks will invariably be present in a true child of God. They will not be perfect until glory, but they will be present now. We cannot afford to be fooled, imagining ourselves saved when we are not. This is a most desperately dangerous condition to be in and a devastating conclusion to draw. We do not need to be confused, either always doubting or building on a wrong foundation. We can know whether or not we are saved. John writes so that we can be sure, knowing ourselves saved and enjoying eternal life.

If these indispensable indications, these marks of a true believer, are not in your heart and life, then you are not a Christian, whatever you claim or imagine, and you should not fool yourself nor dishonor Christ by claiming His name without walking in His ways. You blaspheme Jesus and expose Him to scorn by taking the label of a true believer but living apart from His gracious power and saving wisdom. The hypocrite gives other unbelieving men a reason to scorn and deride true religion by pretending to have what he does not. We see this written on a large scale when those professing to be a true church depart from the truth, teach their own concoctions, live without godliness, and give occasion for others to blaspheme. "Call that Christianity?" they sneer. No! No, it is not Christianity—it is an empty masquerade that gives opportunity for sinners to deride or despair of Jesus, which leaves your hands with the blood of men upon them and which will ultimately damn you if you are not saved from it. It is better to know yourself outside than falsely to imagine yourself inside. You must therefore flee to Jesus and acknowledge your need, repent of your sin, and trust in the Savior.

But if the marks of a child of God are present in you and true of you, then you are a Christian, and you should not dishonor Christ by denying the source of the grace that is in you. Some doubting and fearful saints are terrified that they will lay claim to God's grace in Christ without having it and walk in shadow if not in darkness, robbed of joy and neither being blessed nor blessing others as they might. But consider: these things simply do not grow in the soil of the unregenerate heart, and to possess them without a Christian testimony is to know the privileges of the kingdom without wearing its livery. It might give the impression to some that the fruits of grace can grow in natural soil and imply that unconverted people can attain to true godliness and genuinely Christian morality and therefore prompt a despising of the work of God's Spirit. Others might be profoundly discouraged, imagining that a person can show marks of true holiness but not really be saved and then wonder if they can ever truly testify, "I am His, and He is mine." Friend, if you have these things in you, then honor the God who put them there by owning yourself saved of God and live accordingly.

> *Search me, O God, and know my heart;*
> *Try me, and know my anxieties;*
> *And see if there is any wicked way in me,*
> *And lead me in the way everlasting.* (Ps. 139:23–24)

If you need Jesus, go to Him now, and you will be saved. If you have Jesus—if He has you—then hold fast, love Him, serve Him, and rejoice in Him, for you are a child of God, and He will keep you to the end, perfecting that which He has begun in you.

For Further Reflection

1. List the inconclusive indications concerning the possession of everlasting life. Would you wish to add any more? Have you been building your assurance out of these materials?

2. What might be the different experiences of repentance and faith for someone who has grown up under the sound of the gospel and someone who grew up without hearing the gospel until later in life?

3. What is the difference between regret and repentance?

4. What does faith do for salvation?

5. What are your perceptions of God and of yourself, and what difference has it made in your attitude to God, yourself, and your life?

6. Explain why growth in holiness is an indication of genuine conversion. Take into account the need for discernible progress rather than present perfection.

7. Growth in holiness consists in positive and negative elements. What are they, and why are both important?

8. Why do true Christians love other Christians? Do you find anything of this love in yourself?

9. In what way does false assurance dishonor Christ? How might genuine faith without true assurance dishonor Christ?

Chapter 7

A WORK IN PROGRESS

A gospel that has no "therefore" is a truncated gospel. The gospel has both its sweeping indicatives (statements of objective fact) and its related imperatives (commands to obedient duty). While we face a constant danger of trying to smuggle works back into a relationship of grace, this intimate, grace-soaked, indicative-imperative connection is not the same thing, and we face an equal danger of losing sight of the truth that saving faith works out in a life of principled obedience to the God of grace. The antidote to legalism is not a few drops of license, nor vice versa.

In Philippians 2 the apostle Paul is spelling out the logical connection between the work of Christ for us and the work of Christ in us, the life we have in Christ and the life we live for Christ. The Lord Jesus Himself became obedient to the point of death by the painful and shameful means of the cross, the final point in the terrible downward trajectory of His selfless service to others: "Therefore God also has highly exalted Him and given Him the name which is above every name, that at the name of Jesus every knee should bow, of those in heaven, and of those on earth, and of those under the earth, and that every tongue should confess that Jesus Christ is Lord, to the glory of God the Father" (Phil. 2:9–11). It is on the basis of this sequence that the apostle goes on to make the application to the church in Philippi: "Therefore, my beloved, as you have always obeyed, not as in my presence only, but now much more in my absence, work out your own salvation with fear and trembling; for it is God who works in you both to will and to do for His good pleasure" (Phil. 2:12–13).

Before we go further, let me make one thing plain: nothing in these verses even hints at any contribution by the sinner to Christ's atoning work; nothing suggests that we make any contribution by means of our own efforts to our right standing before the Holy One. Salvation considered as a work *for us* is finished and perfected through the life, death, and resurrection of our Lord Jesus Christ, but—and this is Paul's point—salvation as a work *in us* is still ongoing.

The Context in Which Paul Writes

In Philippians 2:12, Paul is writing to Christians; this exhortation would make no sense if it were directed to unconverted men and women. These are Paul's "beloved" who are working out their "own salvation," a salvation they already possess. Paul is dealing with, is urging upon us, the Christian's response to Christ's example of humility and obedience, with the reality of His exaltation and supremacy—the Father's reaction to that same humble obedience. These are the people who have embraced the person and are called to follow the example, and Paul commends them for their labors to date, having observed their efforts with his own eyes.

But Paul, as a wise pastor, also urges upon them continued effort in this life of principled obedience, not just when he is present "but now much more in my absence." When Paul's eye is not upon them, when his own example is not before them, when his encouragements are not ringing in their ears, they must press on. He cannot be with them personally all the time and shouldn't need to be.

We grapple always with a danger of living before men, being more concerned with what people think than with what God knows. This temptation is present with every believer, perhaps more so when God grants a degree of prominence—the sense of a need to maintain a reputation, to keep up appearances. Furthermore, particular circumstances or the charisma or influence of a particular leader can call forth an attitude or prompt attainments that fade and fail when the circumstances change or the leader moves on. How often do we go into the spiritually intense environment of a Christian conference and come away "pumped up," only to find that the zest and vim of the occasion dissipate quickly once the grind of real life has been wearing on us for a few hours or days? How often do we see a man or woman, by means of his or her character, hold an organization or a group profitably together, setting a high standard and aiming at a righteous goal, only for those around to sink back to a more comfortable level once that holy prompting is removed? Perhaps one of the most horrible scriptural examples is that of King Joash. "Joash was seven years old when he became king, and he reigned forty years in Jerusalem. His mother's name was Zibiah of Beersheba. Joash did what was right in the sight of the LORD all the days of Jehoiada the priest" (2 Chron. 24:1–2). Under the benign influence of Jehoiada, young Joash walked in the ways of the Lord, but Jehoiada could not be his guide forever: "Jehoiada grew old and was full of days, and he died; he was one hundred and thirty years old when he died. And they buried him in the City of David among the kings, because he had done good in Israel, both toward God and His house" (2 Chron. 24:15–16). After Jehoiada's death, Joash came under new influences and turned from God to idols, coming then under the judgment of God. The Lord in His kindness sent prophets to warn Joash, but they were not heeded. Finally He sent faithful Jehoiada's faithful son:

> Then the Spirit of God came upon Zechariah the son of Jehoiada the priest, who stood above the people, and said to them, "Thus says God: 'Why do you transgress the commandments of the LORD, so that you cannot prosper? Because you have forsaken the LORD, He also has forsaken you.'" So they conspired against him, and at the command of the king they stoned him with stones in the court of the house of the LORD. Thus Joash the king did not remember the kindness which Jehoiada his father had done to him, but

killed his son; and as he died, he said, "The LORD look on it, and repay!" (2 Chron. 24:20–22)

Joash gave all the appearance of faithfulness to God while under Jehoiada's godly influence. However, it was not long after Jehoiada's death that Joash proved unfaithful to Jehoiada and to the God that Jehoiada proclaimed. Attachment to an individual does not sustain in the same way as attachment to God and His revelation.

Therefore, Paul does not want the men and women of Philippi to be subject merely to circumstance and charisma and prove themselves false, but rather to be wedded to the truth and the life that flows from it. He wants the saints to live before God, not men. He has already made the plea: "Only let your conduct be worthy of the gospel of Christ, so that whether I come and see you or am absent, I may hear of your affairs, that you stand fast in one spirit, with one mind striving together for the faith of the gospel, and not in any way terrified by your adversaries, which is to them a proof of perdition, but to you of salvation, and that from God" (Phil. 1:27–28). This potent charge does not apply only in public. Obedience to God is not a matter of performance for the eyes of other people, a smoke screen to the eyes of God, or a temporary blip in an otherwise vain career. It is the way of all true believers at all times and under all circumstances. Therefore Paul speaks to all the saints in the Philippian church—and, by extension, to us—and calls us to a life of obedience.

The Command Paul Issues

With this in his mind, the apostle tells these Christians what it means to go on walking before God as their Savior did in a spirit of humble, trusting, ready obedience. It means to "work out your own salvation with fear and trembling."

Consider *the striving* involved. Paul is commanding us to go on working this out, to be continually about this business. It is a call to take great pains with something, to strive against all laziness and distraction by embracing a vigorous and energetic attitude, by cultivating a habit of spiritual diligence. It means to continue to the end, to the full, to be still standing when the battle is done, to use the martial language he elsewhere employs: "Therefore take up the whole armor of God, that you may be able to withstand in the evil day, and having done all, to stand" (Eph. 6:13). It is not a call to occasional endeavor but a command constantly and thoroughly to work at a task until the point of completion. This command neither ignores grace nor abuses it, neither denies it nor runs counter to it. It is a call to men and women in whom grace is powerfully operating, but not a call to "let go and let God." It is a rallying cry to a new creature in Christ to stir up all the faculties of his redeemed humanity and to concentrate them on one object: to pursue the ongoing transformation which is dependent upon and flows from a saved sinner's union with the Son of God.

This is *the substance* of Paul's command: "work out your own salvation." Again, consider that Paul calls the Philippians to work with regard to a salvation they already possess but still need to pursue. It is not a command to *work for* salvation or to *work up* salvation, but to *work out* what God is working in. Romans 8:29 reveals the divine aim of the gospel purposes of God in His redeemed ones: "For whom He foreknew, He also predestined to be conformed to the image of His Son, that He might be the firstborn among many brethren." Conformity to the image of the incarnate Son of God, to the praise of the Lord's glorious grace, is God's intention for us. The foundation has been laid—we are new creatures in Christ—but while the old has gone, the new has come and keeps on coming. Salvation occurs in our thinking, feeling, willing, and doing. We have been liberated to obey, serving God our Redeemer, and we are to use our freedom to that end. There is no contradiction between freedom and duty; rather, the one provides for the other.

Paul speaks of the complete course of our life, the entirety of our calling, of bringing that principle of new life to permeate the whole to ensure that the influences and implications of God's grace in the Lord Jesus characterize everything about us—the realities of that new creation taking ever fuller and more evident effect. It is the destruction of sin and the cultivation of holiness—that indispensable mark of a true child of God—with a view to complete conformity to the Christ.

We are, in this, something like Joshua once possession of Canaan had been assured: the land is ours, but there are many enemies left to be rooted out. Like the town of Mansoul under the rule of Emmanuel in John Bunyan's *The Holy War,* now that the Prince has taken up residence, there is work to be done to bring the corporation into conformity to his rule:

> When the town of Mansoul had thus far rid themselves of their enemies, and of the troublers of their peace, in the next place a strict commandment was given out, that yet my Lord Will-be-will should, with Diligence his man, search for, and do his best to apprehend what town Diabolonians were yet left alive in Mansoul. The names of several of them were, Mr. Fooling, Mr. Let-good-slip, Mr. Slavishfear, Mr. Nolove, Mr. Mistrust, Mr. Flesh, and Mr. Sloth. It was also commanded that he should apprehend Mr. Evil-Questioning's children that he left behind him, and that they should demolish his house. The children that he left behind him were these: Mr. Doubt, and he was his eldest son; the next to him was Legal-life, Unbelief, Wrong-thoughts-of-Christ, Clip-promise, Carnal-sense, Live-by-feeling, Self-love. All these he had by one wife, and her name was No-hope; she was the kinswoman of old Incredulity, for he was her uncle; and when her father, old Dark, was dead, he took her and brought her up, and when she was marriageable, he gave her to this old Evil-questioning to wife.

Bunyan then goes on to describe how Lord Will-be-will executes his commission "with great Diligence," his servant, and the language is of vigorous and decided action. He identifies various sins and compromises to be hunted down and slain: Fooling is hung up, and Let-good-slip (the idea is probably of one who allows good to go by undone) is executed. Clip-promise, one who trims and compromises the promises of God, is pilloried, whipped, and hanged till dead. Carnal-sense is imprisoned, but he escapes and continues to haunt the town, despite great rewards offered and constant efforts to slay him. Wrong-thoughts-of-Christ is imprisoned, where he dies a slow and lingering death. Self-love is imprisoned but then spared because he has so many allies, until "Self-denial stood up, and said, if such villains as these may be winked at in Mansoul, I will lay down my commission. He also took him from the crowd, and had him among his soldiers, and there he was brained. But some in Mansoul muttered at it, though none durst speak plainly, because Emmanuel was in town. But this brave act of Captain Self-denial came to the Prince's ears, so he sent for him, and made him a Lord in Mansoul."

Lord Self-denial then sets about the work with a vengeance, pursuing the Diabolonians with Lord Will-be-will. Together they capture Live-by-feeling and Legal-life, who both die in prison. Mr. Unbelief manages to escape their clutches, for he "was a nimble Jack: him they could never lay hold of, though they attempted to do it often." However, such is the success of the campaign against remaining sin that any wickedness that raises its head is very quickly identified and pursued with the intention of destroying it forever. "And now," reports Bunyan,

> did Mansoul arrive to some good degree of peace and quiet; her Prince also did abide within her borders; her captains, also, and her soldiers did their duties; and Mansoul minded her trade that she had with the country that was afar off; also she was busy in her manufacture.
>
> When the town of Mansoul had thus far rid themselves of so many of their enemies, and the troublers of their peace, the Prince sent to them, and appointed a day wherein he would, at the market-place, meet the whole people, and there give them in charge concerning some further matters, that, if observed, would tend to their further safety and comfort and to the condemnation and destruction of their home-bred Diabolonians.[1]

1. John Bunyan, *The Holy War*, in *The Works of John Bunyan*, ed. *George Offor* (Edinburgh: Banner of Truth, 1991), 3:369–70.

Here, then, is a graphic depiction of what it means for a true believer to hunt down and root out the foul and unwelcome sins that still cling to him, even though he is redeemed in Christ.

Christians will be of little true use to other believers and of limited use in bringing the gospel to bear upon others still outside the kingdom unless their own graces are being vigorously cultivated. But it is all too easy when we read of this kind of battle to think of other people who could really do with paying attention to this kind of instruction—but Paul gives it to you and me. I am to take heed; this is my first point of concentration, for without this all efforts to encourage others will seem (and perhaps will be) mere criticism or cajoling. I cannot help, serve, or model these things until I myself am striving for godliness in the right spirit.

And what is *the spirit* in which this ought to be pursued? The work is to be done "with fear and trembling." People of our age—including many Christians—immediately react to such language with revulsion and opposition, as if for a believer to be characterized by fear and trembling is to live under some dark legalistic cloud, to exist in a state of semi- or entire slavery, to be under law and not under grace. Nothing could be further from the truth!

This is not a slavish fear, the constant terror of being lost or of losing one's standing with God. Rather, it is the very air that the assured saint breathes. It is the holy fear of God's sons, the holy reverence of God's servants, a spirit the very opposite of drowsiness and dullness. It is the spirit of a person who is conscious of being before the living God and who has a proper dread of offending the Lord who bought us, a person who so loves Him that he or she fears to grieve and distress Him in anything. It is what Calvin and others had in mind when they spoke of people living in *coram Deo*—in the presence of the living God of heaven and earth, before His shining face and conscious of His burning eye upon us, expressing something of our own deficiency and therefore acknowledging our dependence, desiring to bring praise and glory to His holy and majestic name. In his commentary on Malachi, Baruch Maoz assesses God's question through His servant Malachi:

"A son honors his father,
And a servant his master.
If then I am the Father,
Where is My honor?
And if I am a Master,
Where is My reverence²?
Says the LORD of hosts
To you priests who despise My name.
Yet you say, 'In what way have we despised Your name?'" (1:6).

Maoz picks up the language of honor and fear, pointing out that "fear is not an attitude of craven humiliation nor is it the terror evoked by the presence of powerful evil" but rather "a combination of affectionate love and deep respect, joined to an awareness of majesty." He insists that we "cannot honor God without lovingly respecting him, without recognizing his glorious majesty. The fear of God is always affectionate. Love of God is always deeply respectful."[3] Commenting further on Malachi 2:5, Maoz assures us that "there is room for fear in our worship. There is room for a lively recognition of the majesty of God's holiness, of his amazing power, of his astounding, disturbing, attractive eternity. There is room for us to tremble at his presence." But it is not just that there is a space for godly fear in our worship of God—we need to have such holy fear. "Where no fear of God is to be found, there is no recognition of his greatness. Worship becomes a form of entertainment…. There is no real adoration of God."[4]

Paul himself knew what it was to be animated by this spirit. This is what he has primarily in mind when he speaks of his disposition among the Corinthians, this consciousness of his dependence on the Lord before whom and for whom he labored: "For I determined not to know anything among you except Jesus Christ and Him crucified. I was with you in weakness, in fear,

---

2. This word is often translated "fear" and gives us the same sense.

3. Baruch Maoz, *Malachi: A Prophet in Times of Despair* (Bloomington, Ind.: Crossbooks, 2012), 21–22.

4. Maoz, *Malachi*, 53.

and in much trembling. And my speech and my preaching were not with persuasive words of human wisdom, but in demonstration of the Spirit and of power, that your faith should not be in the wisdom of men but in the power of God" (1 Cor. 2:2–5). He refers to the same spirit galvanizing him in his second letter to the Corinthians: "Therefore we make it our aim, whether present or absent, to be well pleasing to Him. For we must all appear before the judgment seat of Christ, that each one may receive the things done in the body, according to what he has done, whether good or bad. Knowing, therefore, the terror of the Lord, we persuade men; but we are well known to God, and I also trust are well known in your consciences" (2 Cor. 5:9–11).

Paul also called others to serve with the same disposition: "Bondservants, be obedient to those who are your masters according to the flesh, with fear and trembling, in sincerity of heart, as to Christ; not with eyeservice, as men-pleasers, but as bondservants of Christ, doing the will of God from the heart, with goodwill doing service, as to the Lord, and not to men, knowing that whatever good anyone does, he will receive the same from the Lord, whether he is a slave or free" (Eph. 6:5–8).

He uses this language in this same context of pursuing holiness to the Corinthian church, having laid out the gracious heart and purposes of God toward them: "Therefore, having these promises, beloved, let us cleanse ourselves from all filthiness of the flesh and spirit, perfecting holiness in the fear of God" (2 Cor. 7:1).

We find it as the characteristic stance of saints both under the old and new covenants. For example, the psalmist calls us to be wise:

> *Now therefore, be wise, O kings;*
> *Be instructed, you judges of the earth.*
> *Serve the LORD with fear,*
> *And rejoice with trembling.* (Ps. 2:10–11)

Peter also urges the saints to behave under the influence of the same mind: "And if you call on the Father, who without partiality judges according to each one's work, conduct yourselves throughout the time of your stay here in fear; knowing that you were not redeemed with corruptible things, like silver or gold, from your aimless conduct received by tradition from your fathers, but with the precious blood of Christ, as of a lamb without blemish and without spot" (1 Peter 1:17–19).

But to return to Paul: we may not like it that he consistently uses this language or that he uses it as he does in Philippians 2. It may cut across our expectations and our accustomed usage. It may seem to contradict our most cherished notions. But it cannot be denied, and it does not for one moment undermine or detract from the fact that we rejoice in sins forgiven as those who have been constituted righteous in His sight and brought into His family, having received the adoption as sons. Paul says, as it were, "Even though I should be absent, the living God is ever present. Do not serve as before men, but unto God, conscious of His eye, in a spirit that will give substance, direction, integrity, and humility to all your willing obedience."

This is not a call to sinless perfection but to the earnest pursuit of godliness. It is why Paul goes on to write in this way:

> Not that I have already attained, or am already perfected; but I press on, that I may lay hold of that for which Christ Jesus has also laid hold of me. Brethren, I do not count myself to have apprehended; but one thing I do, forgetting those things which are behind and reaching forward to those things which are ahead, I press toward the goal for the prize of the upward call of God in Christ Jesus.
>
> Therefore let us, as many as are mature, have this mind; and if in anything you think otherwise, God will reveal even this to you. (Phil. 3:12–15)

This is the declaration of a man who is working out his salvation with fear and trembling and who longs to see others committed to the same standards and ends. For a professing Christian to live in a state of persistent and habitual disobedience, contrary to the light of the gospel, is not mere immaturity; it is an absolute absurdity and gives the lie to a person's profession. The Christian works—he presses on.

At this point, we may feel utterly crushed, for this remains a massive demand. Who does not look within his heart and find all manner of idols still contending for a place—sometimes for *the* place—on the throne? The weight of this presses down upon us. Every true believer feels something of this battle and cries out under it: "O wretched man that I am! Who will deliver me from this body of death?" (Rom. 7:24). How can I do this? Where shall I find the strength for such a life? Is there any hope of progress—let alone of final success?

The Confidence Paul Gives

The answer to the last question is a resounding yes! Paul is not so much imposing a burden here as lifting one. There is a happy union between the design of the saving God and the desire of the saved man. When God tells us that we have been saved to be conformed to the image of Christ, the believer calls out, "Praise the Lord!"—for nothing could more delight or animate his soul.

Again, here we see the vital importance of grasping our identity in Christ. Sinclair Ferguson makes this connection in an article on the mortification of sin. Taking Colossians 3 as his starting point, he contends,

> First of all, Paul underlines how important it is for us to be familiar with our new identity in Christ (3:1–4). How often when we fail spiritually we lament that we forgot who we really are—Christ's. We have a new identity. We are no longer "in Adam," but "in Christ"; no longer in the flesh, but in the Spirit; no longer dominated by the old creation but living in the new (Rom. 5:12–21; 8:9; 2 Cor. 5:17). Paul takes time to expound this. We have died with Christ (Col. 3:3; we have even been buried with Christ, 2:12); we have been raised with Him (3:1), and our life is hidden with Him (3:3). Indeed, so united to Christ are we that Christ will not appear in glory without us (3:4).

Failure to deal with the presence of sin can often be traced back to spiritual amnesia, forgetfulness of our new, true, real identity. As a believer I am someone who has been delivered from the dominion of sin and who therefore is free and motivated to fight against the remnants of sin's army in my heart.

Principle number one, then, is: Know, rest in, think through, and act upon your new identity—you are in Christ.[5]

So here in Philippians 2 the apostle is providing us with the theological foundation for his exhortation. This command does not go out in a vacuum but assumes an environment in which believers, having been justified by faith, "have peace with God through our Lord Jesus Christ, through whom also we have access by faith into this grace in which we stand, and rejoice in hope of the glory of God" (Rom. 5:1–2). Our working is built upon and relies upon the prior and continuing work of God in our hearts. This drives a sword into the heart of all boasting, for supernatural and saving grace is at work. Your labor will not be in vain, but you will not get the glory of it, but God will, for He is the One who supplies the vital power for the accomplishment of the things at which you work; who is your all-sufficient strength; who has in Christ, by the Spirit, provided a living well springing up for you to drink and live. This is the process described in Galatians 5: "I say then: Walk in the Spirit, and you shall not fulfill the lust of the flesh. For the flesh lusts against the Spirit, and the Spirit against the flesh; and these are contrary to one another, so that you do not do the things that you wish. But if you are led by the Spirit, you are not under the law" (vv. 16–18). As ever, Paul does not leave such exhortations in the realm of the potentially theoretical. He is speaking of "adultery, fornication, uncleanness, lewdness, idolatry, sorcery, hatred, contentions, jealousies, outbursts of wrath, selfish ambitions, dissensions, heresies, envy, murders, drunkenness, revelries, and the like" (vv. 19–21),

---

5. Sinclair Ferguson, "How to Mortify Sin," *Ligonier Ministries* (blog), http://www.ligonier.org/blog/how-mortify-sin/.

underlining that indulgence in such godliness cuts us off from the kingdom of God. By contrast, "the fruit of the Spirit is love, joy, peace, longsuffering, kindness, goodness, faithfulness, gentleness, self-control" (vv. 22–23). Paul is again telling us to walk in the Spirit as those living in and led by the Spirit, crucifying the flesh with its passions and desires. It is God who is working in us both to will and to do for His good pleasure.

Observe, then, that God is at work in the saints, first, to *will* His good pleasure. As a result of the Holy Spirit's work in our hearts, we hate sin and desire holiness. All volition to do good, all determination to obey, all holy resolve and purpose are the result of God's work in renewing the heart. We would have no desires for godliness if the Lord did not put them in us. But our God does far more, for mere desire without the hope of accomplishment would be a recipe for crippling despair.

Then, God is also at work in the saints to *do* His good pleasure. The cause has its intended effect. Volition gives way to action. Determination leads to execution. Holy resolves issue in holy accomplishments. There is a divine operation that underpins, provides for, and prompts all our laboring for His glory. God is at work both in the willing and doing of what is righteous; He gives the motive and power by means of which saints work out what God has worked and is working in.

The pattern of the whole process is "His good pleasure." It all flows from God's unmerited goodness. His good will is the source of all our good work, and His final goal is our complete salvation: "He who has begun a good work in you will complete it until the day of Jesus Christ" (Phil. 1:6). Consider again that Romans 8:29–30 tells us that God is determined to see us made holy as He is holy, is delighted to see us gradually conformed to the image of His beloved Son, an increasingly perfected likeness to Jesus: "For whom He foreknew, He also predestined to be conformed to the image of His Son, that He might be the firstborn among many brethren. Moreover whom He predestined, these He also called; whom He called, these He also justified; and whom He justified, these He also glorified." Our joy and blessing as God's children are bound up in God's ultimate purpose for us, and He is sovereignly bringing it to pass.

Paul does not say that if you work hard you can in any way contribute to your salvation. Neither, though, does he say that if God is at work, you do not need to bother. Because God is at work, the child of God works, in parallel with and in dependence upon the God who has begun and will complete the work in him. Again, Paul models this himself in his statements in Philippians 3:12: "Not that I have already attained, or am already perfected; but I press on, that I may lay hold of that for which Christ Jesus has also laid hold of me." Such an understanding breeds not so much a prescribed course of action as a particular kind of person—one who sets out to know and do the will of God. The house of Jacob is being called to possess its possessions (Obad. 1:17)—to take hold of what has been made theirs, to work out what God is working in.

This is a challenge for every child of God. Attending a conference, reading a book, spending time with a particularly healthy saint: Will these lead to a temporary push, a peak in effort that passes swiftly away? Or will these principles grip our souls day by day and week by week? Will we see this attitude, not as something that belongs to übersaints or as an expression of a legal spirit, but the typical disposition of a healthy saint, the means of grace feeding and sustaining this disposition in the weekly rhythm of particular communion with God? Will these realities give us a new consciousness of God's grace constantly at work in and upon us, God's Spirit residing in our hearts, God's presence and power with us, leading to a life of willing and principled obedience?

I hope no one who is reading this book needs to stop working. That is, I hope that you are not working at the wrong thing and for the wrong reasons—working for salvation. If you are still seeking to do that, you need to stop working and start looking to Christ: "Look to Me and be saved." Put your work in its proper place: be saved by grace through faith alone, and your gracious and God-dependent working at the salvation you then possess will assuredly follow. And it will all be of grace, and the God of salvation will get all the glory for what He is willing and working in you and what you are willing and working out for Him.

For Further Reflection

1. Salvation as a work for us and salvation as a work in us—what is the difference?

2. Why is it so important to remember that Paul's exhortation to work out our own salvation with fear and trembling is directed to Christians?

3. What temptations do you face to live before men rather than God in the matter of Christian obedience?

4. What does a Christian aim at in working out his or her own salvation?

5. Read again Bunyan's summary of the ongoing cleansing of Mansoul. Which Diabolonians do you need to root out and put out in your own life?

6. Explain Paul's language of "fear and trembling." Why is this an appropriate spirit for a new covenant believer in working out salvation, and what does it look like in practice?

7. What is the relationship between our union with the Lord Jesus and our ongoing battle for holiness?

8. Where do the desire for godliness and the power to pursue it come from? What is the relationship between God's work in us and our working out our salvation? How do these things encourage and stimulate the believer?

Chapter 8

A LIFE IN REVIEW

*W*hen Paul comes to the last act of his life as a bondservant of Jesus Christ, he writes a final charge to his "beloved son" in the faith, Timothy (2 Tim. 1:2). Ever since Paul had come face to face with the risen Jesus on the road to Damascus, seeing and believing, his fundamental disposition had become one of eager, earnest, humble, wholehearted, and obedient service, his life reflecting the answer to the question, "Lord, what do you want me to do?" (Acts 9:6).

Enlisted and commissioned by the Lord Christ, Paul has discharged his duty faithfully and is now passing on the baton with this profound and sober charge to Timothy to hold fast to the truth and to fulfill his ministry. One can only imagine how Paul might have spoken these words and how Timothy might have read them:

> I charge you therefore before God and the Lord Jesus Christ, who will judge the living and the dead at His appearing and His kingdom: Preach the word! Be ready in season and out of season. Convince, rebuke, exhort, with all longsuffering and teaching. For the time will come when they will not endure sound doctrine, but according to their own desires, because they have itching ears, they will heap up for themselves teachers; and they will turn their ears away from the truth, and be turned aside to fables. But you be watchful in all things, endure afflictions, do the work of an evangelist, fulfill your ministry. (2 Tim. 4:1–5)

The backdrop to these words is that the sun is already setting on Paul's life, and the sky is blood-red. There is no peaceful end for this man, no lazy retirement, no enjoying the sight of his protégé excelling. Instead, Paul's life retains his fundamental character to the end: he has lived and will die as a slave of Christ, and therefore he goes not cold, dull, nor empty but full of faith and hope and love.

This character and labor are deliberately placed behind the charge. His life and approaching death enforce his words, both in the manner in which he speaks them and the manner in which he intends them to be heard: "For I am already being poured out as a drink offering, and the time of my departure is at hand. I have fought the good fight, I have finished the race, I have kept the faith. Finally, there is laid up for me the crown of righteousness, which the Lord, the righteous Judge, will give to me on that Day, and not to me only but also to all who have loved His appearing" (2 Tim. 4:6–8). In these verses Paul looks around, looks back, and looks ahead, and the sights he sees push his charge deep into Timothy's conscience.

Looking Around

The picture provided in 2 Timothy 4 is essentially a grim one. Here is the weary old apostle, deserted by those upon whom he believed he could rely, sacrificing for the sake of the gospel some of his most faithful helpers, asking for his cloak because he feels the cold in the so-often-battered-and-bruised flesh of his body, still wanting to keep up his reading and feeling deprived of his books, isolated in facing assaults on his person and faith. It is a profoundly human portrait, one that evokes profound sympathy.

As he considers his circumstances, the apostle reaches his sober conclusion: that he is being poured out as a drink offering and will soon leave this earth. He has always viewed his ministry—and indeed, every life lived for Christ Jesus—as a sacrifice. We find him using this language repeatedly to characterize the life of a believer. To the Romans, he spoke with passionate intensity: "I beseech you therefore, brethren, by the mercies of God, that you present your bodies a living sacrifice, holy, acceptable to God, which is your reasonable service. And do not be conformed to this world, but be transformed by the renewing of your mind, that you may prove what is that good and acceptable and perfect will of God" (Rom. 12:1–2). The same sense of service swims into view when he considers his apostolic labors as a whole, as one who was "a minister of Jesus Christ to the Gentiles, ministering the gospel of God, that the offering of the Gentiles might be acceptable, sanctified by the Holy Spirit" (Rom. 15:16).

He has also used the illustration of a drink offering before in another prison letter with the possibility of death beginning to coalesce in his mind. Writing to the Philippians, he spoke with the same sense, though with less certainty: "Yes, and if I am being poured out as a drink offering on the sacrifice and service of your faith, I am glad and rejoice with you all" (2:17). The imagery comes from temple ritual, in which one of the last elements of the sacrificial rite was the pouring out of the drink offering, as described, for example, in Numbers 15:1–10. As Paul sits in another prison contemplating the far greater likelihood of martyrdom, resonating with all the implications of sacrifice, he sees himself approaching the final element of a life of sacrificial obedience. In his life he has suffered for Christ's sake, offering himself freely, and that sacrifice of self, begun long ago, drawn out over many years, is now being completed.

He is convinced that the final stage is imminent: "the time of my departure is at hand." This is an astoundingly gentle word for a potentially brutal end. It has overtones in it of a soldier breaking camp, striking his tent in readiness to move on. It is sometimes used of a ship weighing anchor as it prepares to leave its present harbor to begin its voyage. The Roman authorities might intend to snuff out his life, but Paul says that this is not the end in any final sense—this is only a departure, a decisive moving on, a heading home at last. Indeed, he has always desired to depart and to be with Christ, which is far better (Phil. 1:23).

We see even here a likeness to our Lord Jesus Christ: Paul has performed a life of Christ-centered, Christlike service; he continues to undergo Christ-inspired, Christlike sufferings. Like his Savior, he has no gentle end, but, like his Savior and because of his Savior, he dies in faith, knowing whom he has believed and is persuaded that Messiah is able to keep that which Paul has committed to Him with a view to the last day. The Puritan Thomas Goodwin died saying, "Ah, is this dying? How I have dreaded as an enemy this smiling friend." To Paul, the present circumstances are the final sacrificial act of a sacrificial career, and he faces them with faith. It is only faith in God's Word, the Word Incarnate and the Word written, that enables such a calm appraisal of such grim prospects.

Looking Back

Having contemplated his present circumstances, Paul now casts his eye back over his life since his enlistment as a bondservant of Jesus all those years ago on the Damascus road and makes three statements about the manner of his life: "I have fought the good fight, I have finished the race, I have kept the faith" (2 Tim. 4:7).

There are two somewhat technical things that we should note about all three of these statements. First, all three verbs are in the perfect tense, which has a durative aspect. By this I simply mean that these are not completed works, now over and done. Rather, they are ongoing works: Paul is still fighting, finishing, and keeping. The effort is being maintained and will continue to the last, to his final breath. Second, the emphasis in Paul's Greek is not where it is in our English translations. In English, we might get the impression of egotism, as if Paul is drawing attention to himself: "I...I...I...." But this is not what Paul writes or what he intends to communicate. Rather, he says, in effect, "The good fight I have been and am still fighting; the race I have been and am still finishing; the faith I have been and am still keeping." If you asked him, "What is this life about, Paul? Is it about *your* fighting, *your* finishing, *your* keeping?" he would reply, "No, not at all. The focus, the aim, the matters of first importance are the fight, the race, and the faith. *Those* are the things that count for us all." So what is the apostle's testimony?

"The good fight I have been and am still fighting." This is a *good* fight, a good contest. There is nothing better, nothing so noble, as this holy struggle. It is worth every scrap of the effort it demands, and it demands every scrap of effort. The word both for the contest itself and for Paul's engagement in it is at the root of our English word *agony*. Paul is telling us that this has been a costly battle. The image is of one of those athletic events of which Paul seems so fond: here it is a wrestling match in which Paul has been pitched against a powerful foe, calling forth prodigious and intense engagement, an effort that he has to maintain at the present hour and expects to maintain every hour to the end.

"The race I have been and am still finishing." Here is another familiar Pauline image. We find it in Philippians 3:12: "Not that I have already attained, or am already perfected; but I press on, that I may lay hold of that for which Christ Jesus has also laid hold of me." We find it in 1 Corinthians: "Do you not know that those who run in a race all run, but one receives the prize? Run in such a way that you may obtain it" (9:24). It is also employed in Hebrews 12: "Therefore we also, since we are surrounded by so great a cloud of witnesses, let us lay aside every weight, and the sin which so easily ensnares us, and let us run with endurance the race that is set before us" (v. 1). In every instance the implication is of a long-distance race.

I recall at school that our cross-country runs used to involve heading down to a local park which would generally be deep in the kind of mud in which small boys have been known to disappear forever. Much of the course, such as it was, lay through fairly dense wood and brush. Disappearing from the teacher's view, the vast majority of the boys would immediately drop their pace, shambling through the cold and filth, until we broke cover what seemed like hours later with the finish line now in sight. As we exited the trees and entered the teacher's field of vision once more, it was amazing what heels were picked up and what speed was generated.

But Paul is not suggesting that he has put in the occasional impressive sprint when he thought someone was watching. The race, as Paul has engaged in it, has always been about running and finishing well, and now the apostle smiles because he sees the finish line not far ahead, the termination of the course. He has had his eyes fixed all along on the goal, the glory of God in the salvation of sinners, among whom he knows himself to be chief:

> And I went up by revelation, and communicated to them that gospel which I preach among the Gentiles, but privately to those who were of reputation, lest by any means I might run, or had run, in vain. (Gal. 2:2)

> You ran well. Who hindered you from obeying the truth? (Gal. 5:7)

> Do all things without complaining and disputing, that you may become blameless and harmless, children of God without fault in the midst of a crooked and perverse generation, among whom you shine as lights in the world, holding fast the word of life, so that I may rejoice in the day of Christ that I have not run in vain or labored in vain. (Phil. 2:14–16)

> To the weak I became as weak, that I might win the weak. I have become all things to all men, that I might by all means save some. Now this I do for the gospel's sake, that I may be partaker of it with you.
> Do you not know that those who run in a race all run, but one receives the prize? Run in such a way that you may obtain it. (1 Cor. 9:22–24)

> Therefore we also, since we are surrounded by so great a cloud of witnesses, let us lay aside every weight, and the sin which so easily ensnares us, and let us run with endurance the race that is set before us, looking unto Jesus, the author and finisher of our faith, who for the joy that was set before Him endured the cross, despising the shame, and has sat down at the right hand of the throne of God. (Heb. 12:1–2)

Paul is at the end of his race and is praying that he might not have run in vain.

"The faith I have been and am still keeping." Now this man of God drops the metaphors and speaks plainly. The truth ought to be more precious to us than anything that can be placed in competition with it, as it was with Paul. Paul has guarded well the great treasure of gospel verities, the unsearchable riches of Jesus Christ. He has held fast to and faithfully declared the saving truth committed to him not through any human channel but "through the revelation of Jesus Christ" (Gal. 1:12), as "a chosen vessel of Mine to bear My name before Gentiles, kings, and the children of Israel" (Acts 9:15). He has not held any of it back, watered it down, edited it, been ashamed of it, added to it, or altered it but has held to it and relied upon it personally and has declared the whole counsel of God to those to whom he was sent.

This is what Paul sees as he surveys the landscape of his past life. These are the contours of his years, with their mountains and valleys, their peaks and troughs, through which this straight path unerringly cuts. Amid all the record of toils, trials, and triumphs, this is the tricolor that flies over Paul's life: fighting, finishing, faithful. And what is now left for this truehearted servant of Jesus Christ?

Looking Ahead

Paul writes, "Finally, there is laid up for me the crown of righteousness, which the Lord, the righteous Judge, will give to me on that Day, and not to me only but also to all who have loved His appearing" (2 Tim. 4:8). Paul sees *a great crown*. Consider what he goes on to say in 2 Timothy 4:18: "And the Lord will deliver me from every evil work and preserve me for His heavenly kingdom." He will be delivered and preserved: this is the crown which has been set aside for Paul, reserved in heaven for him. This is the inheritance appointed for those who are kept by the power of God through faith for salvation (1 Peter 1:3–5). No one can deprive Paul of this crown; this victory wreath is most assuredly his. But notice the quality of this crown: it is "the crown of righteousness."

Again, Paul turns to the athletic arena, in which each discipline had a crown associated with it. The victorious runner took the crown of running, the triumphant wrestler took the crown of wrestling, and so on and so forth. The reward was intimately bound up in the nature of the competition. So this crown—this victory wreath—is given to the one who triumphs in righteousness, not simply the imputed righteousness of Christ in justification but the actively pursued Christlike righteousness of sanctification. Righteousness and righteousness alone—a life of devoted obedience to the Lord Christ—entitles us to and prepares us for our reception and enjoyment of the crown of righteousness, and that crown is reserved for that fighting man until the victory is won.

But Paul also sees *a great Christ*. It is Christ Himself who will dispense this prize, and how quickly and readily do Paul's eyes rise from the prize to the prize giver. He is like a young woman who is engaged or married in cultures where a ring is given. The ring may be of great value or largely worthless, but it is not the ring which so entrances her or makes her heart beat fast, but the one who places it on her finger. It was this rapturous sense that Samuel Rutherford captured, recorded in a hymn drawing on his words:

> *The bride eyes not her garment,*
> *But her dear Bridegroom's face;*
> *I will not gaze at glory*
> *But on my King of grace.*
> *Not at the crown He giveth*
> *But on His pierced hand;*
> *The Lamb is all the glory*
> *Of Emmanuel's land.*[1]

Can we not almost hear the words that the Lord might speak with joy and love as He places the crown of righteousness on His bondservant's brow: "Well done, good and faithful servant; you have been faithful over a few things, I will make you ruler over

---

1. Anne Ross Cousin, "The Sands of Time Are Sinking." Though Cousin wrote the verse, she based it on Samuel Rutherford's sentiment.

many things. Enter into the joy of your lord" (Matt. 25:23)? The bondservant has been identified with Christ from the outset; he is called by Christ, trusts in Christ, has been united to Christ, made an heir with Christ in the family of God, serves for Christ, bears the name of Christ, suffers with Christ, and dies in Christ, eventually sitting with Christ in glory: "To him who overcomes I will grant to sit with Me on My throne, as I also overcame and sat down with My Father on His throne" (Rev. 3:21). The career of a bond slave is utterly Christ-centered. He is the righteous Judge, and in the day of His return He will judge all men and apportion what they deserve. Paul has always served with this day in mind, both for himself and for those to whom he preaches:

> For what is our hope, or joy, or crown of rejoicing? Is it not even you in the presence of our Lord Jesus Christ at His coming? For you are our glory and joy.
> …Now may our God and Father Himself, and our Lord Jesus Christ, direct our way to you. And may the Lord make you increase and abound in love to one another and to all, just as we do to you, so that He may establish your hearts blameless in holiness before our God and Father at the coming of our Lord Jesus Christ with all His saints. (1 Thess. 2:19–20; 3:11–13)

This is the day in which all afflictions will be over, all assaults on the church finished, all the afflicters and assaulters punished in full. Christ will make right every wrong and recompense all and every suffering for His sake. Nothing shall escape His righteous judgment, both for the blessing of the righteous and the condemnation of the wicked. Both His people and His enemies shall be subject to Him.

But Paul also foresees *a great company*. He will not wear such a crown alone and be isolated in that day. To whom else will Christ distribute these eternal crowns? "To all who have loved His appearing." Paul has been an eminent bond slave, but he does not restrict this blessing to those who have matched him stride for stride, done all he did, seen so many converts, and suffered as much. Rather, the whole is still and always centered in the Lord Jesus. The righteous Judge will give a crown of righteousness to all who have loved His appearing. The implication is clear: those who love Christ's appearing are those who live righteously in the light of Christ's appearing. All who live godly in Christ Jesus will suffer persecution, but that same happy band, each one, will receive their crowns at the pierced hand of Jesus Himself: "For the grace of God that brings salvation has appeared to all men, teaching us that, denying ungodliness and worldly lusts, we should live soberly, righteously, and godly in the present age, looking for the blessed hope and glorious appearing of our great God and Savior Jesus Christ, who gave Himself for us, that He might redeem us from every lawless deed and purify for Himself His own special people, zealous for good works" (Titus 2:11–14).

This love of His appearing is the love that dwells with faith— the faith that Christ is now seated at His Father's right hand, waiting till all His enemies are made His footstool to return at the appointed time—and longs for His certain appearing: "To those who eagerly wait for Him He will appear a second time, apart from sin, for salvation" (Heb. 9:28). These are the men and women, boys and girls, who are devoted not to this world but to the next, who are possessed of the only motivation for living righteously in this present evil age: "Beloved, now we are children of God; and it has not yet been revealed what we shall be, but we know that when He is revealed, we shall be like Him, for we shall see Him as He is. And everyone who has this hope in Him purifies himself, just as He is pure" (1 John 3:2–3). This love, too, is spoken of with that enduring sense; these are the ones who endure like Paul—having begun to love, they go on loving Christ's appearing. It inspires them continually, and therefore they go on fighting the good fight, finishing the race, keeping the faith.

What lessons there are for us in this sketch of the apostle as he sits contemplating present, past, and future! Surely we are reminded that the life of bond service to the Lord Jesus is not an easy life, not a life that ever has been or can be expected to become easy. The battle must be fought to the bitter end. There is no lazy dotage for saints. Though the sphere of our combat may shift as our life advances, there is no retirement from spiritual warfare. Our rest does not come in this life but in the life which is to come. No one retires from Christian warfare—we only get promoted. To be sure, there are ways to obtain temporary and apparent respite. We can fudge the issues, conform to the world, and avoid the distinctive witness of sound words with a holy life which always invites the scorn and hatred of the enemies of the cross in some measure—but not if we have our eyes fixed on the Lord Jesus, and our hearts are taken up with an earnest longing for His appearing:

> Therefore, since all these things will be dissolved, what manner of persons ought you to be in holy conduct and godliness, looking for and hastening the coming of the day of God, because of which the heavens will be dissolved, being on fire, and the elements will melt with fervent heat? Nevertheless we, according to His promise, look for new heavens and a new earth in which righteousness dwells.
>
> Therefore, beloved, looking forward to these things, be diligent to be found by Him in peace, without spot and blameless; and consider that the longsuffering of our Lord is salvation." (2 Peter 3:11–15)

Furthermore, surely we must ask ourselves, "What will my retrospective moments be like? As I look back over the contours of my service, what will I perceive? What colors will fly over my life?" If God grants you the opportunity, what will you see? What do you see now? The only way to assure a view like Paul's is to live for Christ now. Surely you do not want to look back with regrets at your life. Will you remember the stand you wish you had taken? Will you think of all the words you wish you had spoken? Will you think with grief of the sinful habits formed and never broken? Of the holy habits neglected or laid aside? Will you mourn over the people to whom you might have spoken the truth or the books you might have read that would have guided you into the truth? Or, even taking into account your sins and failings, will you take a holy and proper satisfaction in the fight in which the Lord sustained you, the race in which you were kept from growing weary, and the faith that kept your eyes and heart fixed on the Lord? This will not happen unless we begin now to lay aside every weight and the sin that so easily ensnares us and run with endurance the race that is set before us (Heb. 12:1–2). Are you living so as to be ready to die? Are you serving so as to have the contentment of a true bond servant of Jesus Christ?

But what of the prospects? Are they not glorious? Perhaps some reading these words are older in years, and the crown of righteousness is almost within reach. You may not have a blood-red sunset, but you can set your younger brothers and sisters an example to the very last. Will you set the standard, and will you show those following how to enter into the joy of your Lord? What glories belong to the saints, and they are nearer to you than to some others of us, by the ordinary measure of things. Each evening you have pitched your "moving tent a day's march nearer home,"[2] and those of us who are younger in years might envy your nearly finished race. Be like that old saint who said, "I am so near the finishing line that I cannot help running with all my might." What example will you leave? Will you be able to charge others to live as you have lived, or will you be ashamed to do so? Such a legacy is not reserved for a spiritual aristocracy but can be passed on by every faithful child of God.

But perhaps you are younger, and you stand in the light of Paul's example as his charge echoes down the years to us. You too are called to consider that you stand before God and the Lord Jesus Christ, who will judge the living and the dead at His appearing and His kingdom. Perhaps you will not preach the word, but you must hear and obey it. You must do all your holy duty in season and out of season, contending in times and places where there is no appetite for faithful, searching, encouraging, instructive ministry. You too, in your own place, must be watchful in all things,

---

2. James Montgomery, "Forever with the Lord!"

endure afflictions, do the work committed to your charge, fulfill your calling.

So what kind of disciple are you? What kind of hearer and doer are you? What is your present witness of fierce attachment to the Lord Christ? Those who have gone before us bequeath us a heritage. How will we respond?

A poem in Old English called *The Battle of Maldon* is the unfinished record of how, in the tenth century, a force of Vikings tried to land at Maldon in Essex after a series of raids along the coast. The Anglo-Saxon force which goes to confront the enemy is led by an earl called Byrhtnoth. The Vikings offer Byrhtnoth a deal: if he will pay them off, they will withdraw. The earl rejects the compromise—it would in itself be an admission of defeat—with a proper scorn. Byrhtnoth eventually allows the Vikings to gather their forces on the mainland to face his cohorts in battle, and at first the Essex men stand firm against the invaders. Eventually, however, Byrhtnoth is killed by a poisoned spear. Now comes the test. Who will run, and who will stand? Some of the leaders flee, one riding on Byrhtnoth's horse, thereby unsettling the defenders and causing others to run. But others stay to rally the troops with a call to unrelenting faithfulness, and they continue to fight to the last man, standing by the body of their lord and eventually falling with him.

However we are meant to interpret the poem and its characters, such an example is a potent challenge. When a man like Paul falls—when the exemplary saints to whom we now look for guidance and direction fall—will we be ready to stand, to take their place and continue the fight? Sadly, there are many who run when the battle grows fierce, often unsettling others in their flight. Let us pray God that we might not be among them but might go on fighting, finishing, and faithful.

To be sure, the way seems hard and long. It seems that way because it is that way, but the Lord never lied to us. There is a cross before a crown, but "the Spirit Himself bears witness with our spirit that we are children of God, and if children, then heirs—heirs of God and joint heirs with Christ, if indeed we suffer with Him, that we may also be glorified together" (Rom. 8:16–17). There will be a crown for the saints of God, a glorious reward dispensed by the hand of the Lord Jesus to all who have served Him faithfully.

And so I close by asking this: Are you on this way? Are you one who has looked to Jesus and been saved? Are you united by faith to the Lord Jesus with unbreakable bonds? Have you come into possession of the unsearchable riches of Christ? Are you made a son of God Almighty, with all the associated privileges and promises? Do you know that sweet assurance that you are a child of God? Are you living and loving as one who belongs to your Lord, marked by growing godliness in every area of life? Are you striving to be the man or woman of God whom you are called to be? Are you working out what God is working in? What does your life look like in retrospect? What does it look like in prospect?

Are you one who has begun to love and continues to love the appearing of our Lord and Savior Jesus Christ? Is that the day in the light of which you are living? Is your life hidden with Christ in God, beyond the reach of harm? Does your life manifest that righteousness demonstrated by those who love and serve their sovereign Lord?

If not, you will have no crown, no heaven, no glory with Him. Those who live in Christ love His appearing. They have died with Him and risen to newness of life. They suffer with Him, looking for that glorious day when they will be glorified together with Him. Will the righteous Judge come to crown you—or to condemn you and consign you to the everlasting flames? The way to begin is to look to Him and be saved, for He is God, and there is no other. The way to continue is to fix your eyes upon Him, looking to Jesus as the author and finisher of your faith. The way to end is with your eyes fixed upon Him still, awaiting from your Beloved the crown of righteousness, which He will give to all who love His appearing, and live in the light of it. And what will you do with that crown? You will do with it what the twenty-four elders do when glory and honor and thanks are ascribed to Him who "sits on the throne, who lives forever and ever": they "fall down before Him who sits on the throne and worship Him who lives forever and ever, and cast their crowns before the throne, saying:

> *'You are worthy, O Lord,*
> *To receive glory and honor and power;*
> *For You created all things,*
> *And by Your will they exist and were created.'"*
> (Rev. 4:9–11)

> *Finish, then, Thy new creation;*
> *Pure and spotless let us be.*
> *Let us see Thy great salvation*
> *Perfectly restored in Thee;*
> *Changed from glory into glory,*
> *Till in heaven we take our place,*
> *Till we cast our crowns before thee,*
> *Lost in wonder, love, and praise.*[3]

This is the end of life in Christ, and—in another and quite wonderful sense—its most glorious beginning.

---

3. Charles Wesley, "Love Divine, All Loves Excelling."

For Further Reflection

1. How does Paul's language help us to understand the sacrificial nature of a Christian's life in relation to Christ?

2. Summarize the tricolor that flies over the contours of Paul's long life journey.

3. Describe the reward to which Paul looks forward. What makes it so precious? Does it seem precious to you, and for what reasons?

4. To whom else is the crown of righteousness promised? What is the connection between loving Christ's appearing and receiving this crown?

5. If you had to write it now, what do you think an honest retrospective of your life would be?

6. Taking into account your age and Christian maturity, how should you respond to Paul's example?

7. What changes might or must you make now in order to end your life more like Paul?